Chic&Easy
Beading

Edited by Alice Korach

KALMBACH
BOOKS

Acknowledgements
Mindy Brooks, Pam O'Connor, Louise Malcolm, Linda Salow, Wendy Witchner, Lisa Schroeder, Carole Ross, Patti Keipe, Tonya Limberg, Bill Zuback, Jim Forbes, Terri Field, Kellie Jaeger, Carrie Rohloff, Lisa Bergman, Maureen Schimmel, and Lora Groszkiewicz.

Printed in the United States of America

04 05 06 07 08 09 10 11 12 13   10 9 8 7 6 5 4 3

Publisher's Cataloging-in-Publication
(Provided by Quality Books, Inc.)

Chic & easy beading / edited by Alice Korach.
    p. cm.
    Chic and easy beading
    Includes index.
    ISBN 0-89024-438-3

    1. Beadwork. 2. Jewelry making.   I. Korach, Alice.
  II. Title: Chic and easy beading

TT860.C48 2004   745.594'2
                        QBI03-200813

Art Director: Kristi Ludwig

Cover photo: Bill Zuback

introduction

Can any woman ever have too much jewelry?... I ask myself every morning when I pull open the shallow drawers in my dresser to choose the day's finery. "No," I assure myself, "as long as oysters keep making pearls, the earth compresses minerals into gemstones, and artists craft magnificent metal and glass beads, there can never be such a thing as too much jewelry." In the 1990s, three remarkable things happened that changed many of our lives for good. These three events also vastly enriched our sense of self and our innate creativity. Abrams published *The New Beadwork* by Kathlyn Moss and Alice Scherer (1992), *Bead&Button* Magazine was born (1994), and a new kind of bead store started springing up all over the United States fueled by a never-before-seen, fabulous array of beads from all over the world that made it easy to create fashionable and fine jewelry.

Beading had come into its own as an art form and an irresistible hobby for women and men from all cultures and walks of life. If you can pass a needle through a hole, you can make almost all of the jewelry in this book in a matter of minutes or only a few hours. The projects included in this volume consist of a few that were previously published in *Bead&Button* and a great many that we, the editors of the magazine, designed especially for our two *Chic&Easy* annuals. We chose designs that ran the gamut from classical and always in style, through ethnic, casual, glitzy, and timely fashions. And since we made every single piece of jewelry shown here, we were able to show you all the details of construction with numerous process photos. The directions are fully tested and can be relied on for accuracy.

You may not be able to find precisely the beads shown in some of the projects because bead availability is constantly changing. So enjoy the challenge of making these designs your own by choosing beads of the same size but a different color or shape. One of the most remarkable things about beading is how it unleashes the creativity you may not know you possess. If you really love a particular bead, it will almost certainly look great on you. Truly, the hardest part of creating bead jewelry is choosing among the many beautiful beads.

So enjoy. Stringing your own bead jewelry just might change your life, making you happier, calmer, and more self-fulfilled. It's done just that for all of us at *Bead&Button* Magazine.

contents

Introduction 3

Basics of bead stringing 8
by the Editors
Identify the key tools and materials
you need to make beaded jewelry

Basics 136
Explore technical know-how

Tips & techniques 140
Learn more efficient approaches

Index 144

necklaces

Italian designer necklace 10
by Hannah Marie Deutschendorf
Make a simple multi-strand design,
stunning with or without a pendant

Keep it simple 16
by Emily Quinn
Use seed beads to create easy
multi-strand necklaces

Drop everything! 18
by Sue Raasch
Enhance a chain necklace with
wrapped-loop dangles

Showcasing lampwork beads 22
by Fae Mellichamp
Create a multi-strand necklace that
features a trio of beads

Lariats, a fashion basic 26
by Mindy Brooks
String a fun lariat in either stones
or seed beads

Shimmer aplenty 34
by Pam O'Connor
Use two colors to make a multi-
strand necklace with sleek appeal

Show it off 36
by Louise Malcolm
Use knots to set off single beads or
clusters meant to be seen

Awl knotting 37
by Louise Malcolm
Practice the classic technique used
to knot together a string of pearls

Making odd ends meet 42
by Adele Clausen
Showcase colorful assorted beads in
a random-pattern necklace

What to do with leftover beads 44
by Nancy Alden
Make dangles in a mix of colors
for a freshwater pearl necklace

String a vintage look 46
by Deb Gottlieb
Add a retro touch to a necklace
with a tassel pendant

Caged beads 48
by Linda Salow
Wrap a bead with silver wire for an
attention-getting pendant

Graceful geometrics 52
by May Frank
Learn cross-needle weaving—a
building-block technique

Chained elegance 56
by Alice Korach
Create a tiered crystal necklace
using chain for spacers

Knot hard 62
by Sarah K. Young
Use tweezers to perfect your skills at bead knotting

Use French wire for a professional look 64
by Deb Gottlieb
Finish your finest work the way professional jewelers do

Beaded links 66
by Jane Baird
Connect your favorite beads with linked wire loops

Easy as 1–2–3 68
by Karen Smaalders
Explore your options with this convertible, three-strand necklace

Summer spirals 72
by Alice Korach
Make an airy-looking choker with wrapped-loop bead caps

Create the tribal look 74
by Karen Smaalders
Bundle multiple strands to make a necklace with ethnic flair

String a lariat with pizzazz 80
by Kelly Charveaux
Turn a centerpiece donut into the loop of a toggle closure

Fine feathered friends 82
by Pam O'Connor
Match your beads with a few feathers for a hip ensemble

Strand multiplication 88
by Pam O'Connor
Add fullness to your stringing with necklace spreaders

Centerpiece elegance 90
by Mindy Brooks
Put your best beads up front and hook them to wire sides

Y wonder 94
by Pam O'Connor
A tassel adds new glamour to a Y-necklace

Contemporary accents 100
by Mindy Brooks
Highlight a multi-strand necklace with art-glass beads

Liquid silver jewelry ensemble 102
by Alice Korach
Create a waterfall of shimmering silver over semi-precious stones

Understated elegance 106
by Alice Korach
String an easy two-hole pearl collar

Asymmetry in stone 108
by Alice Korach
Try a blend of single- and multi-strand techniques

A new look at jeweler's chain 114
by Mindy Brooks
String heavy or sharp beads on durable "foxtail" chain

Falling leaves 116
by Pam O'Connor
String this pearl necklace with a crystal dangle centerpiece

Hooked on pearls 120
by Mindy Brooks
Combine decorative cones with an art bead for an elegant centerpiece

Zigzag floral necklace 126
by Alice Korach
A complicated-looking necklace is made with easy daisy-chain stitch

Oodles of pearls 132
by Alice Korach
Make your own clasp to highlight a multi-strand necklace

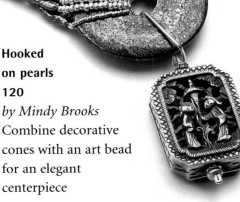

earrings

Hoops are hot 13
by Bette Anthony
Crystals add sparkle to a pair of classic earrings

Chain reaction 28
by May Frank
Wrapped loops star in a creative earring technique

Hoop dangles 29
by Louise Malcolm
Fine wire adds a second row of beads to plain hoops

Bent-wire fantasia 32
by Alice Korach
Create stunning earrings with free-form wire shapes

Cause a stir 41
by Pam O'Connor
Create earrings that move with jointed dangles

Charmed, I'm sure 55
by Alice Korach
Use charms and crystals for special earrings

Cone classics 65
by Pam O'Connor
Create elegant drop earrings with silver cones

Diamond ball earrings on a budget 70
by Alice Korach
Weave crystals into spheres for glittering attention-getters

Chained dangles 77
by Alice Korach
Use almost invisible chain to link dangles to post earrings

Feather weights 82
by Pam O'Connor
Make hip earrings with feathers to tickle your neck

Beaded dangles 84
by Alice Korach
Wrap seed beads around hoop earrings and add fine chains

Teardrop earrings 87
by Mindy Brooks
Emphasize the shape of oblong beads with looped wire

Pearl ribbons 99
by Alice Korach
String pearls and small beads on chain

Liquid silver jewelry ensemble 102
by Alice Korach
String a shimmering loop with multiple strands of silver

Asymmetry in stone 108
by Alice Korach
Make easy dangle earrings with jade and tourmaline beads

Mix and match 111
by Pam O'Connor
Start a fun wardrobe of earrings with your own findings

Falling leaves 116
by Pam O'Connor
String pearls and crystals for sparkling green dangles

Basic to bold 124
by Alice Korach
Apply one simple technique for a variety of earrings

Spiral earrings 135
by Pam O'Connor
Wrap a wire spiral to energize stone dangles

bracelets

Tall or short 14
by Diane Hyde
String heirloom lace on memory wire for fancy cuff bracelets

Time on a beaded strand 20
by Emily Quinn
Beads transform an ordinary department-store watch

Mini-pearl dangle bracelet 25
by Gloria Harris
String dangles in groups to add punch to a simple design

Make your own tennis bracelet 30
by Judi Mullins
Create patterns with crystals as you practice right-angle weave

Interlocking circles 130
by Mindy Brooks
Adapt one cross-needle design
to many styles

other accessories

Pin frills 58
by Pam O'Connor
Add a playful fringe border
to trim a brooch

Classic multi-strand bracelets 38
by Nicolette Stessin
Use toggles, braids, and hidden
knots to enhance a basic design

Toggles, the perfect clasp 40
by Nicolette Stessin
Ring and bar closures are easy and
ideal for bracelets

Lasso your wrist 50
by Pam O'Connor
Make a tasseled lariat bracelet

Unforgettable bracelets 60
by Louise Malcolm
Random or regular, memory wire
cuff bracelets are fun and easy

Elegant pearl lattice 78
by Alice Korach
Create crystal spacer bars for
a classic bracelet

Beaded bangles 84
by Alice Korach
Transform thriftstore bangles
with seed bead wraps

Woven stone cuff 96
by Pam O'Connor
Learn to use a loom and make this
easy, fashionable cuff

Liquid silver jewelry ensemble 102
by Alice Korach
Close strands of shimmering silver
with a toggle clasp

Simply linked 105
by Pam O'Connor
Join a few beads and bits of chain
to make versatile bracelets

Understated elegance 106
by Alice Korach
String an easy bracelet of elegant
two-hole pearls

Asymmetry in stone 108
by Alice Korach
Embellish jade beads
with tourmaline

**Delicate dangle
bracelets 112**
by Alice Korach
Use slides to hang
bead dangles

Appliqué cuff 122
by Alice Korach
Wrap your wrist
with unusual stones

Half-round Roman ring 93
by Alice Korach
Create an elegant ring with
a flat bead and wire

The personal touch 119
by Mindy Brooks
Trim a purchased handbag
with bead embroidery

Winged brooch 128
by Pam O'Connor
Embroider a shimmering
butterfly pin

Basics of bead stringing

The key tools and materials

It's easy to construct beautiful bead jewelry that's as good as or better than the jewelry you see in up-scale department stores. If you can thread a cord or wire through a hole, you're more than halfway there. The big "secret" of the pros is knowing what tools and materials to use to get the best results. All the important tools are shown in the bottom photo on p. 9. As you can see, there aren't many. Stringing materials offer more choices (top photo, p. 9). Your choice depends on the type of beads and their weight and hole quality. It is also dependent on the findings (photo below) that you use to attach a clasp.

findings

Findings are the parts that link beads into a piece of jewelry. Always buy the best metal findings you can afford. If you use base metal, it will soon discolor. Sterling silver and gold-filled findings usually increase the cost of a piece by less than $5 and look good for many years. Here are the key findings:

A. A **head pin** looks like a blunt, long, thick sewing pin. It has a flat or decorated head on one end to keep the beads from falling off. Head pins come in different diameters and lengths ranging from 1-3 in. (2.5-7.6cm).

B. Eye pins are just like head pins except that they have a round loop on one end, instead of a head. You can make your own eye pins from wire or head pins.

C. A **jump ring** is used to connect two loops. It is a small wire circle or oval with a split that you can twist open and closed.

D. Split rings are used like jump rings, but they are much more secure. They look like tiny key rings and are made of springy wire.

E. Crimp beads are small, large-holed, thin-walled metal beads designed to be flattened or crimped into a tight roll. You use them instead of knots when stringing jewelry on flexible beading wire.

F. Bead tips are small metal container beads used to link a cord-strung necklace to a clasp while concealing the knots. (They are sometimes called *calottes*.) They come in either a basket shape or a two-sided, open bead shape. Basket bead tips hold the knot inside the cup. You squeeze the halves of bead-shaped bead tips together with the knot inside. The cord comes out the bottom of both.

G. Clasps come in many sizes and shapes. Some of the most common are the toggle, consisting of a ring and a bar; the lobster claw and the spring ring, which open when you push on a tiny lever; the S-hook, which links two soldered rings or split rings; and the hook and eye.

H. Earrings come in a huge variety of metals and styles, including post, French hook, kidney wire, and hoop. You will almost always want a loop on earring findings so you can attach beads.

I. Cones are usually made of metal and look like pointed ice cream cones with openings at both ends. They are ideal for concealing the ends and knots of a multi-strand necklace and joining it attractively to the clasp.

J. Flexible beading wire comes in several brands. They all consist of very fine wires twisted or braided together and covered with a smooth plastic coating. Aculon (tiger tail) is the stiffest and kinks easily because of the small number of inner wires (7). Beadalon and Soft Flex both have many inner wires (21 or 49, depending on size). They drape well and are relatively kink resistant.

K. Cord is the most common stringing material. It consists of several plied (twisted) finer cords. Bead cord is made in a number of materials, but nylon is the most common, being both

strong and supple. Cord size is indicated either by a number or a letter; the lower the number or letter, the thinner the cord, except for O, which is very thin. Choose a size that will pass through your beads snugly four times, and always string with doubled cord. Pearls are traditionally strung on silk, but many of the new nylons are almost as supple and much less stretchy. Nylon upholstery thread works well, too. Do not string beads on monofilament because it becomes brittle or on sewing thread because it's too weak.

L. *Wire* is used to make loops and eye pins or to wrap beads creatively. The smaller the gauge, the thicker the wire. At top left, we show 16 gauge (thickest), 20 gauge (mid-range), and 24 gauge (thin). Memory wire (the circle) is steel spring wire; it's used for coil bracelets, necklaces, and rings (the bracelet size is shown).

tools

You need very few tools for making bead jewelry, but don't use the large, grooved pliers in your family tool kit; they give terrible results.

M. *Chainnose pliers* for jewelry making have smooth, flat inner jaws, and the tips taper to a point so you can get into tiny spaces. Use them for gripping and for opening and closing loops and rings. Some people call chainnose pliers flatnose because the inside of the jaw is flat.

N. True *flatnose pliers* don't come to a point at the tip, so they can't go everywhere that chainnose pliers can. They are useful but not absolutely necessary.

O. *Roundnose pliers* have smooth, tapered, conical

jaws. You form loops around them. The closer to the tip, the smaller the loop.

P. On *diagonal wire cutters*, the outside (back) of the blades meets squarely, yielding a flat-cut surface. The inside of the blades makes a pointed cut. Always cut wire with the back of the blades against the section you want to use so that the end will be flat. Do not use your jewelry wire cutters on memory wire,

which is extremely hard; use your family's heavy-duty cutters or bend it until it breaks.

Q. If you use crimps often in jewelry making, you'll eventually want a pair of *crimping pliers*. Crimping pliers have two grooves in their jaws to enable you to fold or roll a crimp into a compact shape.

R. An *awl* is the easiest tool to use when knotting between beads.

S. Use *thread snips* for cutting bead-stringing cord. Lightweight, fine-pointed scissors (manicure scissors) or clippers are ideal.

T. *Twisted wire needles* are made from a length of fine wire folded in half and twisted tightly together. They have a large, open eye at the fold, which is easy to thread. The eye flattens when you pull the needle through the first bead. ◉

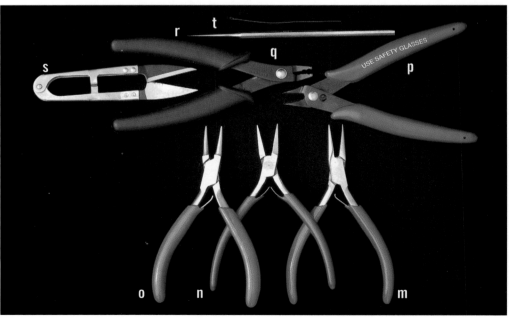

Italian designer necklace

*A simple multi-strand design is stunning
with or without a pendant*

by Hannah Marie Deutschendorf

When I saw an Italian designer's gorgeous multi-strand citrine necklace in a fashion magazine, it was love at first sight. After checking my bank account and realizing, of course, that I couldn't afford the designer necklace, I plunged into making my own version of it.

While selecting the citrine beads for my necklace, I found many other beads that would be perfect for variations on the theme. Pearls, of course, are always appropriate, and a mass of inexpensive freshwater pearls makes a lot of necklace for a relatively small cost. Fire-polished crystals also make a wonderful statement en masse (see the cover photo).

Almost any large bead, pendant, or donut works well for a dressy pendant. When I held my citrine beads next to a large amber donut at my local bead shop, they glowed. The stick pearl pendant on the cover had been one of those things I couldn't resist at a gem show a few months before, and I've long admired Carolyn Driver's glass bead amphoras, at left, (308) 787-9999.

As I was putting the citrine necklace together, I realized that I could wear the necklace with or without the pendant. And when I looked at the wealth of possible pendants I had assembled, I also realized that I could mix and match pendants!

a

b

c

materials

all necklaces

- 12 in. (31cm) ½-in.-wide (1.3cm) Sheer ribbon, gold
- Silamide, nylon upholstery thread, or nylon bead cord, #1 or 2; silk cord for pearls, B or C
- Clasp
- Beading needles, #12 or twisted wire needles
- G-S Hypo cement
- Fray Check (optional)
- Tools: round- and chainnose pliers, diagonal wire cutters

citrine necklace

- **15** Strands 3x5mm citrine rectangular beads
- **1** 2-in. (5cm) Amber donut
- **4** 3mm Gold-filled beads
- **9** Seed beads, any color
- **2** Bead cones/caps, antique gold
- **8** in. (20cm) 20-gauge Gold-filled wire, half-hard

crystal necklace

- **600** 6mm Fire-polished Czech glass crystals
- **48** 2mm Sterling silver or gold-filled beads
- **1** Centerpiece bead or pendant
- **2** 6mm Split rings
- **8** Sterling or gold-filled bead tips

pearl necklace

- **14** 16-in. (41cm) Strands 3-4mm freshwater pearls
- **2** 6mm Split rings
- **8** Sterling or gold-filled bead tips
- **1** Centerpiece bead or pendant

stepbystep

citrine necklace

❶ Cut 4 in. (10cm) of wire and make a wrapped loop with a diameter half the length of the cone so the ends of the strands will be concealed inside. Repeat.

❷ Cut 5 ft. (1.5m) of cord. Thread a needle and double the cord. String a seed bead, leaving a 3-in. (7.6cm) tail. Go through the seed bead again from the same direction for a stop bead. String 22½ in. (57cm) of citrine. Cut the needle from the thread and tie the strand onto one of the wrapped loops with several knots. Repeat 8 more times. Seal the knots with polish. Tie all the ends together before gluing the bunch of knots. When dry, trim to ⅟₁₆ in. (1.6mm).

❸ Remove the stop beads and tie each end onto the other wrapped loop. Finish as in step 2.

❹ Insert the wire through the hole in a cone from the inside. String two 3mm beads on the wire and slide them down to the top of the cone. Make a wrapped loop above the beads, attaching half of the clasp before wrapping the loop. Repeat on the other side (**photo a**).

❺ Bring a ribbon end through the donut and around the front of the strands to the back. Cross the ribbon ends over each other between the donut and strands and bring them around to the front of the necklace. Cross the ends again and bring them around to the back (**photo b**). Tie a square knot (see "Basics," p. 136). Trim the ends and seal with Fray Check.

pearl and crystal necklaces

❶ For the crystal necklace, cut two 5-ft. lengths of bead cord and thread a needle on each. Tie the four ends of the doubled cords together with an overhand knot (see "Basics"). Glue the knot and string through a bead tip to the outside. String three 2mm beads then 18 in. (46cm) of crystals on each doubled cord.

For the pearl necklace, knot together three doubled cords and glue the knot. String through a bead tip and tie the cords together snugly against the bottom of the bead tip with an overhand knot. String 18 in. of pearls on each cord.

❷ End the pair of crystal strands with three 2mm beads. Then string into another bead tip. Cut off the needle. Tighten the cord so it's firm but not rigid and tie a surgeon's knot inside the bead tip (see "Basics"). Glue the knot.

End the pearl strand group by tying them together with an overhand knot tight against the pearls and string-

ing into another bead tip. Finish like the crystal strands (**photo c**).

❸ Make four groups of strands for both necklaces (12 pearl strands, 8 crystal strands), following steps 1 and 2. When the glue is dry on the knots, trim the ends and close the bead tips with chainnose pliers.

❹ Attach a split ring to each clasp end. Then hang the bead tips on the split rings, rolling each bead tip tightly closed with roundnose pliers.

❺ Tie on the centerpiece as in **photo b**, step 5 above. ◖

Hoops are hot

*Crystals add sparkle
to this classic earring*

by Bette Anthony

Not long ago, a box of high school-era treasures from the early seventies resurfaced in my home. There, along with my yearbook, a few diaries full of long-forgotten secrets, and an ex-boyfriend's identification bracelet, was a pair of hoop earrings. It had been a long time since I'd seen those earrings, and they inspired me. Hoops are more popular and available today than they've been in years.

The hoop earrings shown here are a sophisticated update of the simple gold hoops I used to wear in high school.

stepbystep

String a pair of fine-gauge hoop earrings with fire-polished crystals for sparkle

materials

- 1 Pair 1¼ in. (3.2cm) hoop beading earrings, gold-filled
- **2** Strands 3mm Czech fire-polished crystals
- 14 3mm Cube-shaped pewter beads, gold-finished
- 18 4mm Bicone crystals
- 14 5mm Bicone crystals
- 14 4mm Soldered jump rings, gold-filled
- 14 Thin head pins, gold-filled
- Tools: Round- and chainnose pliers, diagonal wire cutter

and add beaded dangles for color and movement. Change the look and make a lighter earring by using fewer crystals and dangles, as shown in **photo a**.

1 Start by making 7 dangles for each earring. String head pins with crystals and cube-shaped beads as follows:
- one 5mm crystal, 1 pewter bead (make 4)
- one 5mm crystal, 1 pewter bead, one 4mm crystal (make 4)
- one 5mm crystal, 1 pewter bead, two 4mm crystals (make 4)
- one 5mm crystal, 1 pewter bead, three 4mm crystals (make 2)

2 Attach each dangle to a jump ring with a wrapped loop above the last bead on each head pin (see "Basics," p. 136).

3 String seven 3mm crystals onto a 1¼ in.-diameter hoop earring. Add the dangles in the following order and space them with two 3mm fire-polished crystals: 2-bead dangle, 3-bead, 4-bead, 5-bead, 4-bead, 3-bead, 2-bead. Finish by stringing 7 crystal beads onto the end of the hoop.

This covers most of the hoop, leaving just over ¾ in. (2cm) of wire to pass through the earlobe. Use chainnose pliers to pinch the jump rings if they slide over a neighboring bead.

If you're working with a different hoop size, string the hoop with 3mm crystals to obtain the right count, then

a

b

figure out the spacing for your dangles. Take the crystals off the earring and string them again with the dangles in the right positions.

4 Bend the tip of the earring wire at a 90-degree angle, using chainnose pliers to keep the crystals from sliding off (**photo b**).

5 Make the second earring to match the first. ●

Tall or short

String heirloom lace on memory wire for fancy cuff bracelets

by Diane Hyde

Making memory wire bracelets has always driven me crazy. Just threading beads round and round to make a wide enough bracelet is tedious and doesn't satisfy my creative urge to make the most of memory wire.

While looking through my old issues of *Bead&Button* for a new beading project, I found a lovely, lacy seed bead necklace pattern that looked intricate but was actually easy (*B&B* #11, p. 7). I practiced until it was second nature and did samples with different sizes, colors, and types of seed beads. What was I going to do with all these strips, and how could I close the sides? There was the answer on my worktable—memory wire!

stepbystep

Memory wire is steel spring wire. It comes in different coil sizes (ring, bracelet, and necklace) and different gauges. The coarser gauges that are most readily available will accommodate sizes 6º, 8º, and 10º seed beads, triangle beads, and hex beads as well as larger-holed (Japanese) 11º seed beads. I've also had success with Japanese 15º hex beads on finer-gauge memory wire. When choosing beads, make sure that the holes of the picot and spacer beads are large enough to accommodate the wire with a little extra room.

Never use jewelry cutters on memory wire; they will be ruined. Use heavy-duty wire cutters or grasp the wire in your pliers where you want it cut and bend it back and forth until it snaps. Then file the rough edge. If you're planning to end the wire with a loop or a half-drilled bead, filing isn't necesary unless the edge is so rough that it will cut your beading thread.

❶ Cut two identical pieces of memory wire that fit your wrist comfortably with an overlap of about 1 in. (2.5cm). Turn a loop on the last ½ in. (1.3cm) of one end of each wire (see "Basics," p. 136). If you would prefer to omit the end loops, include only half the overlap and glue a half-drilled memory-wire bead onto one end of each wire with cyanoacrylate (Zap-A-Gap) glue. Put a small amount of glue on the end of the wire and quickly slip the stopper bead all the way onto the wire.

❷ Weave a strip of "heirloom lace" as shown in **figures 1** and **2**; weave the starting tail into the lace. Make the strip long enough to go around your wrist plus a little more; measure it against the piece of memory wire. Leave the needle and thread attached.

❸ Feed the first picot at the start end onto one piece of memory wire. Then thread one spacer bead, a 6º, 8º, 10º, or a Japanese 11º, onto the wire. Thread the next picot on this side of the lace then another spacer bead. Repeat about six more times to see how the lace lies and whether you like this spacer bead choice (**photo a**). If the lace seems compacted, try using two spacer beads; if it is too spread, as in **photo a**, use 1 spacer

bead. When you like the look, string the rest of this side in the same manner.

❹ Try the bracelet on after stringing the first side. If the lace is the right length and the bracelet falls where you intended, unstring 3-4 picots and end the lace by running the needle back through 3-4 rows, tying and gluing half hitch knots between beads 2-3 times (see "Basics"). String through 2-3 beads and cut the tail off close. If the lace is a little short or long, unstring 3-4 picots and adjust the length. Then end the thread and restring the beads. Turn a loop or glue a bead at this end.

❺ String the second wire through the other edge of the lace so that it matches the first side.

❻ If you turned loops in the memory wire, make head-pin dangles to hang on them. Put small, simple dangles on the underlap and make longer, multiple dangles for the overlap end (**photo b**). If the beads on the memory wire are too tight when you're finished, crush 1-2 spacer beads with jewelry pliers. Shield your eyes from flying glass particles.

❼ Optional: You can make double- or triple-wide bracelets by cutting one more wire than the number of lace strips. Thread the outer edges of the bracelet as described above, but alternate the picot beads of two adjacent strips on the middle wire. Depending on the size of the beads, you probably won't need spacer beads on the middle wire (**photo c**). ❂

materials

- 2-3 Lengths of bracelet memory wire to fit your wrist plus 1 in. (2.5cm)
- **4-8** Head pins for dangles
- 10g E-beads or 6º seed beads
- 10g 10º or 11º seed beads or crafts store small seed beads
- **4-20** Accent beads and charms for dangles
- Jump rings or split rings to attach charms
- Nymo B or D
- Beading needle, #12
- Beeswax or Thread Heaven
- Clear nail polish to glue knots
- Tools: roundnose pliers, small metal file
- Optional: Zap-A-Gap cyanoacrylate glue and memory wire half-drilled beads

a

b

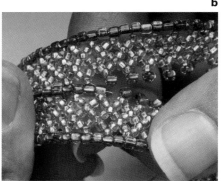

c

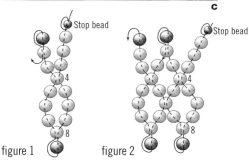

figure 1   figure 2

Figure 1: Tie a stop bead 4 in. (10cm) from the end of a 1-2-yd. (.9-1.8m) thread. String 9 beads. Go through #8 (a picot); string 3. Go through #4. String 3. Go through the next-to-last bead (a picot).

Figure 2: String 3 and go through the middle bead on the first 3-bead group. String 3 and go through #2 (a picot). String 3 and go through the middle bead on the next 3-bead group. String 3 and make a picot. Repeat figure 2 to the desired length.

Keep it simple

Create easy multi-strand necklaces with seed beads

by Emily Quinn

I adore seed beads. These tiny snippets of the rainbow can be bought in abundance cheaply. By hank or by gram, by tube or by pack, however I purchase them, new batches of seed beads always make me feel rich. But I try to keep admiration sessions with my seed bead stash private because an uninitiated observer (like my husband) wouldn't understand my pirate-like glee as I gloat over my horde.

Seed beads are also the workhorse of beads. Used to set off larger, more expensive beads or to weave an off-loom or loomed design, they quietly do the job, calling little attention to themselves. But here are two multi-strand necklace designs in which seed beads grab the limelight. The first features one luscious color of 8º seed beads, and the second uses a colorful assortment of seed bead sizes and a handful of pressed glass beads.

stepbystep

monochrome necklace

❶ Decide how long you want your necklace to be. A standard neckline length is 18 in. (46cm), but you might want to add a few extra beads to allow for the fullness.

❷ Attach a split ring to the loop on each part of the clasp. Split rings open like a key chain ring (split ring pliers are useful for opening the rings). Once you've inserted an end of a split ring in the clasp loop, use your chainnose pliers to turn the ring until it is seated properly (**photo a**).

❸ Attach the hooks of 3 bead tips to each of the split rings with roundnose pliers (see "Basics," p. 136). Subtract the length of the clasp, rings, and bead tips from the finished length to determine the length of your bead strands.

❹ Cut 2 pieces of nylon bead cord 3 times that length, thread a twisted wire needle onto each, and pull the needles to the center of each cord. Tie all four ends together with an overhand knot (see "Basics") and dot the knot with nail polish. Bring both needles through a bead tip from the hook end to the outside (**photo b**).

❺ Now string the correct length of

beads on each strand. String both strands through a bead tip on the other split ring, stringing toward the hook, and cut off the needles. Make sure the beads are snug and tie the cords together with a square knot (**photo c** and "Basics"). Dab the knot with nail polish applied from the tip of a needle and trim the ends when dry. Using chainnose pliers, squeeze the halves of the bead tips together, enclosing the knots (**photo d**).

❻ Repeat steps 4-5 with the next pair of bead tips. Tie three strands together with three needles for the strands between the last pair of bead tips.

multi-color necklace

❶ This necklace is slightly graduated—the second strand is ½ in. (1.3cm) longer than the first and the third strand is 1 in. (2.5cm) longer. Decide on the length of your first strand.

❷ Measure the length of the clasp and split rings and subtract it from the length you chose for the first strand as in step 3 above.

❸ Thread a needle with a cord cut 3 times the finished length of the first strand and tie the ends together with 2-3 overhand knots (see "Basics"). Dab the knots with clear nail polish or glue. When dry, trim the threads and string a bead tip, pulling the knot inside the cup. Close the bead tip with chainnose pliers. Attach the bead tip to one of the split rings as in step 3 above.

❹ String *an 8º seed bead, a 6º seed

bead, an 8º seed bead, and an 11º seed bead*. Repeat from * to * until you reach the desired length.

❺ String a bead tip and finish as in step 5 above. Attach the second bead tip to the other split ring.

❻ Repeat step 3 for the second strand. String * three 11º seed beads and an 8º seed bead*. Repeat from * to * until you have reached the desired length. Finish as in step 5.

❼ Repeat step 3 for the third strand. String *a 6mm Czech glass bead, a 6º seed bead, an 8º seed bead, a 6mm glass bead, an 8º seed bead, and a 6º seed bead*. Repeat from * to * until you have reached the desired length. Finish as in step 5.

❽ Attach the split rings to the clasp. **◉**

materials

for each necklace
- **6** Bead tips
- **1** Clasp
- **2** Large split rings, 6mm
- Nylon bead cord, #0 or 1, in a coordinating color
- Clear nail polish
- Tools: chainnose and roundnose pliers, twisted wire needles, split ring pliers (optional)

monochrome necklace
- 20-30g or 1 Hank 8º seed beads

multi-color necklace
- 10g 11º Seed beads. burgundy
- 10g 8º Seed beads, light amber, purple/iris-lined
- 10g 6º Seed beads, silver-lined matte teal
- **41** 6mm Czech pressed glass beads

a

c

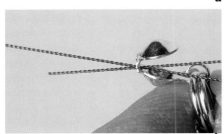

b

d

Drop everything!

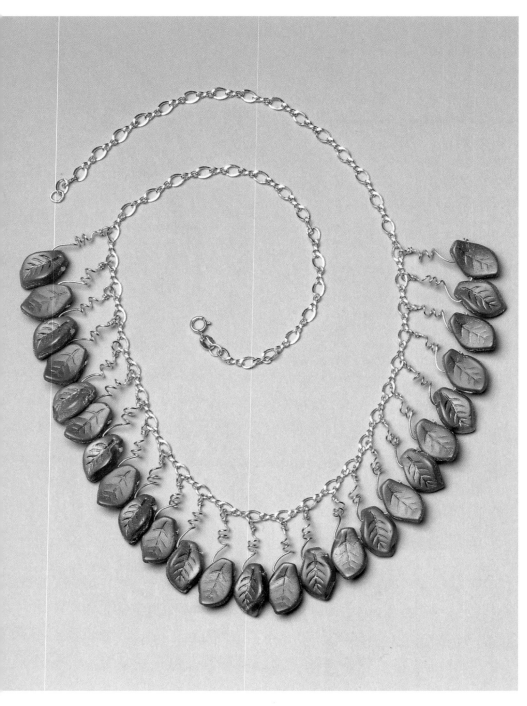

The whimsical necklace of iridescent leaves shown at left is as suitable for an evening out as it is for daytime wear. Change the look by varying the number of dangles or design a mix of leaves and other beads. Then play with the wire to give your dangles an individual twist.

For a quick, traditional version of this necklace, string pearls and/or crystals on head pins and attach them to the chain with a wrapped loop. Once you've mastered the skill of making wrapped loops, the possibilities are limitless.

stepbystep

leaf necklace

If you're new to wire work, practice making the twisted dangles with copper or other inexpensive wire. Since the design is so free-form, you can't really make a mistake. Just don't overwork the wire at any one point or it will break.

❶ String a leaf onto a head pin and slide it against the head. Grip the wire tail with your chainnose pliers or your fingers and pull it gently into an arc over the bead (**photo a**).

❷ Hold the roundnose pliers so the tip points toward the leaf. Use the tip to grab the the head pin about ¼ in. (6mm) away from where the wire exits the bead (**photo b**).

❸ To make the wire spiral, coil the tail around the pliers three times, repositioning the pliers after each half wrap (**photos c** and **d**).

❹ With chainnose pliers, grip the wire right above the spiral and bend it away from the bead at a 90-degree angle (**photo e**). Then, about ¹⁄₁₆ in. (2mm) above the previous angle, bend the wire toward the back, making

Enhance a chain necklace with wrapped loop dangles

by Sue Raasch

another 90-degree angle to start the wrapped loop (**photo f**).

5 Make the first half of a wrapped loop (see "Basics," p. 136).

6 Slip the loop through the chain's-center link and complete the loop.

7 Repeat steps 1-5 to make the required number of dangles. Space them evenly on both sides of the center dangle.

8 Once the dangles are attached, soften the look by stretching the spiral coils slightly with pliers or your fingers.

pearl and crystal necklace

Design these simple dangles to suit the occasion, using pearls or a mix of pearls and crystals (bottom photo).

1 String a pearl and a crystal onto a head pin.

2 Make the first half of a wrapped loop.

3 Attach the dangle to the center link in the chain. Finish the wrapped loop.

4 To complete the necklace, continue to make and attach dangles to the chain. The necklace shown below has 9 dangles spaced about an inch (2.5cm) apart. •

a

d

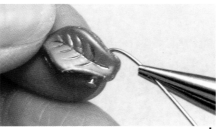

b

e

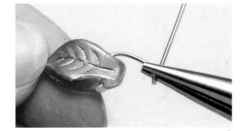

c

f

materials

leaf necklace
- 18 in. (45cm) Silver chain necklace
- **25** Leaf beads with top holes
- **25** or more Silver head pins, medium gauge
- Tools: Round- and chainnose pliers, diagonal wire cutters

pearl and crystal necklace
- 18 in. (45cm) Silver chain necklace
- **9** 6mm Pearls
- **9** 3mm Crystals
- **1** pkg. Ultra-thin silver head pins (Bead-world exclusive, 206-523-0530)
- Tools: Round- and chainnose pliers, diagonal wire cutters

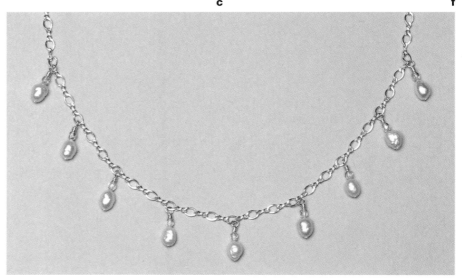

Time on a beaded strand

*Beads transform an ordinary
department-store watch*

by Emily Quinn

U tility is not the sole virtue of this watch. It's also attractive, unique, inexpensive, and easy-to-make. When you check the time, its beauty will ease that momentary panic when you realize, girl, you are LATE!

The project began when I found a watch on sale for a few dollars at a discount store. Its classic gold face with a celestial dial was fastened to a dull watch band and screamed out for a bead makeover.

I took my cue from the gold stars and deep blue of the celestial dial. Soon I had assembled faceted quartz beads, blue cathedral beads, and lapis lazuli beads with a few gold findings and was ready to make the transformation.

stepbystep

A variety of watch attachments and watch faces for beading are available from jewelers' supply companies. If you use a watch face from a department store, measure carefully between the casings for the spring attachment. Most are 12-14mm, but they may be set too deeply for some of the larger, more decorative watch attachments to be inserted. The 3-strand bead bar I used has a small profile that will fit most standard watch faces.

1 Measure your wrist and add ½ in. (1.3cm) of ease for fastening the toggle clasp. To calculate the length of the beaded strands, measure the length of the watch face with the watch attachments. Subtract this total and the length of the toggle from the total bracelet length. Divide by 2 to determine the length of each side.

2 Cut three 12-in. (30cm) lengths of cord and insert one through each hole on the 3-hole watch attachments. Tie them into a loose overhand knot so they won't slip back through the holes. You will untie this knot later to tighten and reknot the strands securely.

materials

- **1** Watch face
- **2** 3-Strand bead bar watch attachments (available at Fire Mountain Gems 800-355-2137 or Jewels Express www.jewelsexpress.com)
- **1** Toggle clasp
- **4** Bead caps
- **6** Cathedral beads
- **12** 7mm Lapis lazuli beads
- **18** 6mm Round, faceted-quartz beads
- **18** 4mm Round, faceted-quartz beads
- **18** 4mm Disc-shaped, faceted-quartz beads
- Nylon bead cord, #3
- G-S Hypo cement
- Twisted wire beading needles

3 When you design your strands, remember to start with small beads at the watch attachment and end with small beads at the bead cap. I used 4mm beads. My symmetrical, tapered design works well with a traditional watch face. However, a more random, casual design also works. To make your strands the right length, string the center strand, including both bead caps and 2 or 3 small beads before the clasp. These beads should be no larger than 6mm to permit the toggle to pivot and fit through the ring. When your bracelet design is the right length, remove the beads up to and including the bead caps. Then string the other two strands to match the beaded length of the middle strand.

4 Once the three strands are the same length, thread the ends through the top of the first bead cap. Only one strand continues through the second bead cap. String 2 or 3 small beads no larger than 6mm and then the toggle or ring of the clasp. Go back through the small beads and the first bead cap (**photo a**). The ends now come out between the two bead caps.

5 Knot the strands tightly in a surgeon's knot (see "Basics," p. 136) against the bead cap closest to the clasp (**photo b**). Glue the knot. After the glue is dry, trim the ends and slide the other bead cap up to cover the knot.

6 Push the beads on the three strands up against the bead cap. Untie the overhand knot. Tie two strands snugly into a surgeon's knot against the watch attachment (**photo c**). Tie the remaining strand and a strand tail from the first knot in another surgeon's knot. Glue the knots. After the glue is dry, trim the tails.

7 Repeat steps 2-6 on the other side.

8 Thread the springs from the watch face into the watch attachment and fit them into each side of the watch face. ●

a

b

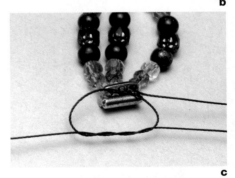
c

Showcasing
lampwork beads

Create a multi-strand necklace that features three beads

by Fae Mellichamp

Many lampworked beads created by contemporary glass bead artists are large, and it can be a challenge to come up with designs that feature them effectively. Since they're often expensive, you may also want your design to highlight a small, affordable quantity of artists' beads. A necklace consisting solely of lampworked beads can also be too heavy to wear comfortably. As a glass beadmaker, I'm always looking for ways to help customers develop designs that feature our beads (Chimera Glass Works) as well as those of other lampwork artists.

The idea for this necklace came from three lampworked beads left over from another project. The inspiration for the wire bobby pins came from a bracelet made by fellow glass bead artist, Pam Dugger of Hollywood, Florida.

stepbystep

Loops of seed beads connect three artist beads, and the back of the necklace is a single strand of pressed glass beads and seed beads. Set aside 50 seed beads in a single color for the two loops that connect the front and back of the necklace. Before using silver or gold wire to make the bobby pin-shaped pieces, practice with copper wire.

bobby pins

❶ Cut 6 wire pieces the length of one lampwork bead plus ¾ in. (2cm), times 2. For example, if the main beads are 1 in. (2.5cm) long, each piece of wire should be about 3½ in. long (9cm).

❷ Position the center of 1 piece of wire in the chainnose pliers' jaws to begin making a loop that will be ⅛-¼ in. (3.2mm-6.4mm) across and bend the wire to form a 90-degree angle (**figure 1**). Shift to the roundnose pliers, placing the top jaw above the bend (**figure 2**).

❸ Grasp the horizontal leg of wire and wrap it over the top jaw, pulling toward you until the legs are parallel (**figure 3**).

❹ Remove the pliers from the partial loop and re-insert them with the bottom jaw through the loop (**figure 4**).

❺ Continue wrapping the same leg under the bottom jaw (**figure 5**).

❻ With the pliers, grasp the wire loop

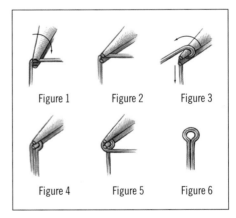

Figure 1   Figure 2   Figure 3

Figure 4   Figure 5   Figure 6

where the two legs cross. Bend down the horizontal leg until it is parellel to the other leg (**figure 6**).

❼ Check the bobby pin's length against the main beads. The legs must be ½ in. (1.3cm) longer than the bead. Make 5 more bobby pins.

necklace

❶ Mix the seed beads and the 4-6mm beads in a bowl. Cut four 60-in. (1.5m) lengths of thread.

❷ Pull a needle to the center of one thread length. Double and knot it at the end, leaving a 1-in. tail. String 24 in. (61cm) of beads from the bowl, spacing the larger beads evenly.

❸ Hold the ends so the beads slide to the center of the thread. Then tie the ends together with a square knot (see "Basics," p. 136), forming a circle of beads that drapes softly (**photo a**).

❹ Take the needle through a few beads and tie a half-hitch knot (see "Basics"). Knot 2-3 more times in this manner. End by going through 3-4 beads. Clip the needle off the thread, pulling the thread taut so it slips into a bead. Use the needle to end the other pair of tails the same way. Glue the knots with nail polish applied from the tip of the needle, but don't create stiff sections. The knots should be as unobtrusive as possible, ideally slipping inside the beads.

❺ Repeat steps 2-4 three more times.

❻ Wrap one of the seed-bead loops evenly around your hand three times. Separate the legs of a bobby pin slightly. Slip the three loops of seed beads over one leg of the bobby pin, catching them in the loop. Push the legs of the bobby pin back together. Dangle the loops

from the bobby pin to ensure that they are equal and move freely (**photo b**).

❼ Slide the legs of the bobby pin through the lampwork bead that goes at the center of the necklace. Using round-nose pliers, curl the ends of the legs, making loops larger than the bead's hole (**photo c**). Form the loops opposite each other and snug against the bead.

❽ Repeat step 6.

❾ Run the second bobby pin with its triple bead loop through the center bead, starting at the end with the two loops. The legs should emerge with one on each side of the loop holding the seed bead loops. Curl the legs into loops (**photo d**).

❿ Attach the two remaining lampwork beads and seed bead loops to the center of the necklace by repeating steps 6-9: Connect the ends of the loops on each side of the center bead to bobby pins that go through the side beads and pin the last two loops to the other side of these beads.

⓫ String 25 of the reserved seed beads onto 16 in. (41cm) of flexible beading wire (for a longer or shorter necklace, adjust the length of wire). String 1 crimp bead. Pass an end of this strand through 1 set of loops then through the crimp bead and pull tight. The length of wire and a 1-in. tail exit the crimp (**photo e**). Secure the crimp. Do not trim the tail.

⓬ String 8 in. (20cm) of beads, making sure the wire tail is inside the first inch of beads. Alternate one kind of pressed glass bead with single seed beads to create the impression of a knotted bead strand (**photo f**).

⓭ String 1 crimp bead and the other 25 reserved seed beads. Pass this section of seed beads through the other end loops of the necklace. Take the wire tail back through the crimp bead and about 1 in. of beads. Pull the wire snug but not so tight that the bead strand becomes stiff. Close the crimp. Carefully trim any excess wire. ●

materials

- 3 Lampworked beads with large holes (Chimera Glass Works, 1520 Merry Oaks Court, Tallahassee, FL 32303; (850) 385-6480; chimera@talweb.com)
- Seed beads, variety of shapes, sizes, and finishes
- 1 8-in. (20cm) Strand pressed-glass beads
- 30 4-6mm Beads, variety of shapes, sizes
- 16 in. (41cm) Flexible beading wire, .014
- 30 in. (76cm) Silver or gold 20-gauge wire, half-hard
- **2-4 Crimp beads**
- Nymo B or Silamide beading thread
- Beading needle, #12 or 13
- Shallow bowl
- Clear nail polish (optional)
- Copper wire (optional)
- Tools: scissors, crimping pliers, round- and chainnose pliers, diagonal wire cutter

a   b

c

d

e

f

Mini-pearl dangle bracelet

*Stringing dangles in
groups adds interest
to a plain design*

by Gloria Harris

Recently, I visited the jewelry department in an upscale department store and saw a bracelet like the one at right for $80. I thought that a bit steep, especially considering how plentiful and inexpensive freshwater pearls are in bead stores. In fact, the selection and quality is often better than in department stores.

stepbystep

The size of your pearls and your wrist will determine how many pattern repeats you'll need. So buy more head pins than you expect to use.

Although you may be tempted to put the dangles on plain loops, don't. They can fall off too easily.

❶ String one small pearl on a head pin and make a small wrapped loop against it (see "Basics," p. 136). Make a lot of these dangles (I used 69). If you plan to begin the bracelet with a long pearl and end it with a group of dangles, make one dangle with a tiny loop that won't slip over a crimp. Put it aside to string last. If you prefer, just begin and end the bracelet with a long pearl.

❷ Put a clip on one end of the wire and string 2 crimp beads. Then string the following repeat: 1 6mm pearl, 3 dangles (**photo a**) until the bracelet goes around your wrist with little or no slack. String the tiny dangle last or end with a 6mm pearl.

❸ String 2 crimp beads and one end of the clasp. I took the jump ring off the

a

b

magnetic clasp and strung through the clasp loop to make sure it would remain securely attached to the beading wire.

❹ Bring the tail of the wire (3-4 in. / 7.6-10cm) back through the two crimps. First crimp the crimp bead next to the clasp. Then crimp the other right against the first (**photo b**). Trim the wire tail. The magnetic clasp tries to stick to your tools, but hold it out in line with the bracelet as best you can.

❺ Attach the other end of the wire to the other clasp part and go back through the two crimp beads. Tighten and crimp as in step 4. ●

materials
6⅝-in. (17cm) bracelet
- **1** Strand (16 in. / 41cm) 4mm nearly round colored pearls
- **1** Strand 6mm elongated pearls
- **18** in. (46cm) Flexible beading wire, .012 or .014
- **4** Tube-style crimp beads
- **1** Magnetic clasp (adds ½ in. / 1.3cm) or any small clasp
- **60-90** Ultra-thin head pins (Beadworld exclusive, 206-523-0530)
- Tools: chain- and roundnose pliers, wire cutter, crimper, and alligator clip or hemostat

Lariats, a fashion basic

String these easy classics in no time

by Mindy Brooks

This year, you've seen lariats around the necks of models, actresses, and divas in materials ranging from ropes of diamonds to strands of pearls to strings of seed beads. What all lariat necklaces have in common is their heritage as the rope lasso used to capture livestock. Certainly, ours have come a long way from the corral.

stepbystep

stone lariat

The green lariat shown at right is made with polished aventurine pebbles. Any small, semi-precious stone beads or pebbles will work, but avoid using stone chips, which often have sharp edges. They can be uncomfortable against the back of your neck.

❶ Thread a twisted wire needle with 5 ft. (1.5m) of beading cord and string 5 in. (13cm) of pebbles. Slide them close to the end of the cord, leaving a 6 in. (15cm) tail. Tie the working thread and tail together to form a loop using a square knot (see "Basics," p. 136) **(photo a)**. Be sure your pendant fits through the loop before tying. Secure the knot with clear nail polish and let it dry. Thread the ends through a few beads before cutting.

❷ Continue to string pebbles until the lariat is long enough to wrap around your neck twice and extend another 8-12 in. (20-30cm) or the length you prefer. My lariat measures 40 in. (1m) from loop to pendant.

❸ Adjust the tension of the strung pebbles and be sure there are no gaps between them. Attach the pendant by wrapping the beading cord through the loop 3 or 4 times. *Take the needle back through several pebbles, make a half-hitch knot (see "Basics") **(photo b)**, and glue the knot with nail polish.* Repeat from * to * twice and go through a few more pebbles before you cut the thread.

❹ To wear the lariat, hold the loop in front of your throat, wrap the lariat around your neck twice, and insert the pendant through the loop.

seed bead lariats

These lariats can be made in a single color or highlighted with beads in a variety of shapes, sizes, and colors.

❶ Thread your needle with 5 yds. (4.6m) of upholstery thread. With the

---

materials

both lariat styles
- Beading cord or nylon upholstery thread
- Twisted wire needles
- Clear nail polish

stone lariat
- **3** 16-in. (41cm) Strands semi-precious stone pebbles
- Art bead or pendant

seed bead lariats
- **2** Hanks 8º seed beads, one or two colors
- Mix of small beads, various shapes and finishes, optional
- Hemostats or alligator clips

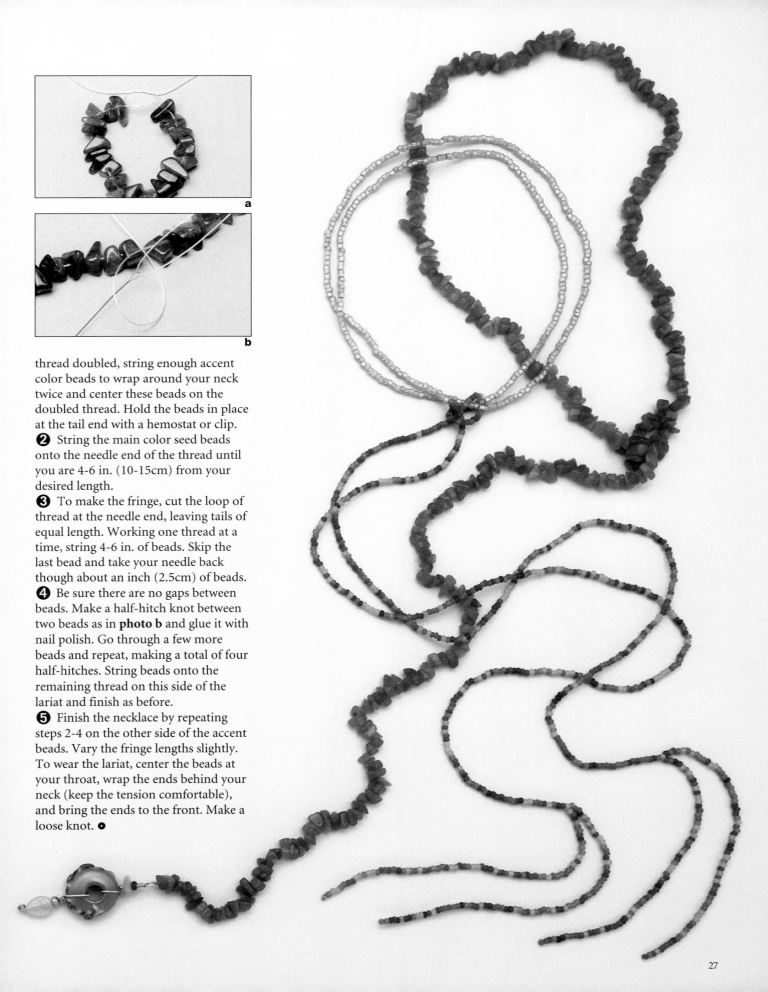

thread doubled, string enough accent
color beads to wrap around your neck
twice and center these beads on the
doubled thread. Hold the beads in place
at the tail end with a hemostat or clip.

❷ String the main color seed beads
onto the needle end of the thread until
you are 4-6 in. (10-15cm) from your
desired length.

❸ To make the fringe, cut the loop of
thread at the needle end, leaving tails of
equal length. Working one thread at a
time, string 4-6 in. of beads. Skip the
last bead and take your needle back
though about an inch (2.5cm) of beads.

❹ Be sure there are no gaps between
beads. Make a half-hitch knot between
two beads as in **photo b** and glue it with
nail polish. Go through a few more
beads and repeat, making a total of four
half-hitches. String beads onto the
remaining thread on this side of the
lariat and finish as before.

❺ Finish the necklace by repeating
steps 2-4 on the other side of the accent
beads. Vary the fringe lengths slightly.
To wear the lariat, center the beads at
your throat, wrap the ends behind your
neck (keep the tension comfortable),
and bring the ends to the front. Make a
loose knot. ❍

Chain reaction

Wrapped loops star in this creative earring technique

by May Frank

No one can argue about how addictive beads are. One look in any beader's closet or studio is proof enough. But I didn't realize how addictive a technique could be until I sat down to make a pair of wrapped-loop earrings.

I started by making the blue crystal earrings shown here. Then I was curious about how other types of beads would look, and I began to experiment. A left-over strand of freshwater pearls quickly became a

beautiful pair of earrings. The same was true for semi-precious stone chips.

In a shorter length, the earrings look very tailored. Adding length makes them more dramatic. Doubling the number of dangles fills out earrings made with smaller beads. And substituting ear wires for posts presents no problems at all.

After playing with a half-dozen variations, I feel like I've just scratched the surface of what's possible with this simple earring technique.

stepbystep

Wrapped wire loops connect crystal beads securely to a cable chain in these delicate earrings. Make yours longer or shorter than mine by adjusting the length of the chain and the corresponding number of dangles.

1 String one bead onto a fine head pin. Place your chainnose pliers about 1⁄16 in. (1.6mm) away from the bead and bend the wire until it forms a right angle. Make the first portion of a wrapped loop (see "Basics," p. 136). Since these earrings are delicate, you'll need to make a small loop that's no bigger than a link in the cable chain. Work close to the pliers' tip where the diameter of the jaws is narrowest.

2 Slip the bottom link of the cable chain into the loop. To complete the wrapped loop, bring the long wire tail around the wire between the crystal and the bottom of the loop about three times, covering that small stem of wire completely. Clip the wire close to the last wrap.

3 Attach one bead to each link in the chain. When you reach the desired length, skip one link and cut the chain.

4 Use one of the medium-gauge head pins or 20-gauge wire to make the loop between the earring post and the chain. Make a wrapped loop attached to the loop on the earring post. Add a bead

materials

- **1** Strand 3-5mm Czech crystals, small pearls, or 3-5mm faceted gemstones
- **50** Fine-gauge sterling silver or gold-filled head pins
- **2** Medium-gauge sterling silver or gold-filled head pins or 20-gauge wire
- 6-8 in. (15-20cm) 2.2mm Sterling silver or gold-filled cable chain
- **1** Pair sterling silver or gold-filled stud earrings with loop
- Tools: diagonal wire cutter, chain- and roundnose pliers

below the wrapped loop. Trim the remaining wire to 3⁄8 in. (1cm) and make a small plain loop (see "Basics") **(photo)**. You can make a wrapped loop if you prefer.

5 Attach the top link of the chain to the plain loop and close the loop. ●

Hoop dangles

Fine wire adds a second row of beads to plain hoops

by Louise Malcolm

Beaded hoop earrings with a row of loops along the bottom for dangle beads have been all the rage this year, but the findings have been impossible to find.

stepbystep

String the beads at the back of the hoop. Then add the supplementary wire and string the dangle portion of the earring. So that the earrings hang well, the front has a few more beads than the back.

❶ If the hook end of the hoop is bent, straighten it with chainnose pliers.

❷ String 8 6º seed beads on the hoop.

❸ Cut a 6-in. (15cm) length of 24- or 26-gauge wire and wrap one end around the hoop in a complete revolution with the tail against the last bead strung. Then bend the wire so it is against the wrap and parallel to the hoop (**photo a**). Clip off the tail flush with the hoop and the last bead.

❹ Choose a large-hole bead and thread it onto the supplementary wire and the hoop wire and push it against the wrap.

❺ Bend the supplementary wire down and back toward the beaded section at about a 60-degree angle (**photo b**).

❻ Wrap the wire around a slightly thicker portion of your roundnose pliers than normal. (You're making a fairly large partial loop, ½ to ⅝ in./1.3-1.6cm, as opposed to the normal ⅜-in./1cm loop.) Be sure to keep the wire evenly

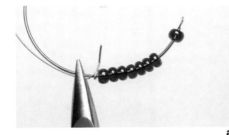

a

b

c

d

e

curved, and stop wrapping when it points toward the hoop closure, slightly past the vertical (**photo c**). Thread on a dagger bead.

❼ Use chainnose pliers to bend the wire so it is parallel to the hoop again (**photo d**), and thread on another large-hole seed bead.

❽ Repeat steps 5-7 until you have hung either 5 or 7 dagger beads.

❾ After threading the bead after the last dagger onto the hoop and wire, wrap the wire tightly around the hoop and clip off the excess (**photo e**).

❿ Thread on about 10 more beads and bend the last ¼ in. (6mm) of the hoop up.

⓫ Make the other earring. ◉

materials

- **1** Pair of 1⅛ in. (2.8cm) beadable hoop earrings
- **1** Small package 6º seed beads, large holes
- **10-14** Dagger beads, 16mm long
- **12** in. (30cm) 24- or 26-Gauge wire, match hoop metal
- Tools: wire cutters, round- and chainnose pliers

Make your own
tennis bracelet

Right-angle weave and crystals fulfill your dreams

by Judi Mullins

My friend, Cheryl Swanda, and I were bemoaning the fact that neither of us would ever own a diamond tennis bracelet. Fortunately, she suggested that we make our own version of those bracelets out of Austrian bicone crystals.

At first, I thought about using bicones for beadweaving, but the shape doesn't lend itself well to that. Then, I tried mentally to fit bicones into different stitches. When I hit right-angle weave, I knew I'd found a good idea. I drew some sketches and showed them to Cheryl, who dropped some crystals in my hand and sent me home.

The crystals took to right-angle weave even better than I'd expected. Their bicone backsides meshed with each other perfectly. I stitched until I'd woven all the crystals into a fabric. It was beautiful but lacked something.

Those of you who design jewelry know the importance of spacer beads. They give the eye a place to rest. Out came my bead stash to find the perfect spacer bead—some simple seed beads. As I wove them into the fabric, it changed before my eyes.

materials (7-in./17.8cm bracelet)

- 144 4mm Bicone crystals, main color
- 32 4mm Crystals, accent color
- 11º or 14º Czech seed beads, accent color
- Nymo B thread
- Beading needles, #12 or 13
- Beeswax
- 2-Strand round filigree clasp
- Clear nail polish

stepbystep

First, make the right-angle-weave fabric for the bracelet. Then embellish it with seed bead spacers.

❶ With 8 yds. (7.3m) of heavily waxed and doubled thread, string 2 main-color crystals, half the clasp, and 2 more crystals, leaving a 3-in. (7.6cm) tail. Tie into a circle with the tail (**photo a**). Apply clear nail polish to the knot and let dry.

❷ Work in right-angle weave (see "Basics," p. 136), following the pattern at right. After adding the eighth set of accent crystals, string 2 main-color crystals, the clasp, and 1 main-color crystal. Make sure the bracelet is not twisted and the clasp is oriented correctly.

❸ To start the second row and complete the clasp attachment, string 1 main-color crystal, the second ring on the clasp and 2 crystals (**figure 1/photo b**). Finish the stitch. Continue working in right-angle weave.

❹ For the last stitch, string 1 crystal, the second ring on the clasp, and 1 crystal (**photo c**). Finish the stitch.

❺ Go back through the bracelet to reinforce it with a 3-bead zigzag thread path (**figure 2**) and add a seed bead in the center of each group of 4 accent beads. Go down one side of the bracelet (red) and up the other side (blue).

❻ After reinforcing, start at one corner and add a seed bead between each crystal on the outer edge. If the seed beads overfill the space between crystals, choose a smaller bead. Turn at the corner (go through the clasp to reinforce it) and add seed beads along the other side of the bracelet. ●

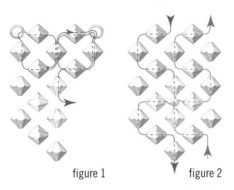

figure 1   figure 2

a

b

c

Bent-wire fantasia

Create stunning earrings with
free-form wire shapes

by Alice Korach

Many women put earrings on in the morning with little more thought than they give to brushing their teeth. But earrings say a lot about you and about how you want to be viewed. They provide small or large, sparkling or plain accents alongside your face just below your eyes and so draw attention to your face, especially your eyes. Simple earrings are a good way to create eye contact and improve communication.

Large or glitzy earrings draw attention to themselves as well as to your eyes. They say that you have presence and self-confidence (even if you don't think you do). If you're feeling very shy, but you need to appear confident, try wearing larger earrings than normal. It's like that song from *The King and I*, "Whenever I feel afraid ... ."

I don't often wear earrings, but when I do, I want them to be special and unusual. I want to assert myself and be a little dramatic. That's why the earrings in this article are some of my favorites. You have total control of their drama quotient. Make extra bends or levels with the wire and hang flashy crystals if you want extra boldness. Make fewer bends and hang quieter, classy pearls to project self-assurance and dignity.

stepbystep

Use the full-size templates for your first two pairs of earrings, then devise your own bent-wire designs. But be sure to practice with copper or base-metal wire before committing your design to sterling or gold wire. Because you wrap wire in tight spaces, the "sleek curves" earrings take a little practice and dexterity.

sleek curves earrings

❶ Cut a 6-in. (15cm) length of 14- or 16-gauge wire. Flush-cut both ends (place the flat back of the wire cutters against the part of the wire you'll use).
❷ Start at the top of the template (**figure 1**) and form a twice-around, slightly open spiral.
❸ Bring the wire out horizontally from the bottom of the spiral so it extends the width of the bead you wish to set in the first loop plus ⅛ in. or so (3-4mm).
❹ Curve the wire around a stick pen, marker, or wooden dowel with a

materials

sleek curves earrings

- 10 in. (25cm) 14- or 16-Gauge sterling silver wire, dead soft
- 1 yd. (.9m) 24-Gauge gold-filled wire, dead soft
- 6 7-8mm Colored pearls
- 6-8 4mm Swarovski bicone crystals
- 2 4mm Colored pearls, optional
- 2 Ultra-fine head pins (Beadworld, 206-523-0530)
- Pair of gold earring findings with loop

chandelier earrings

- 6 in. (15cm) 16-Gauge sterling silver twist wire, dead soft (Thunderbird Supply Co., 800-545-7968)
- 8 Head pins
- 4 in. (10cm) 2.4mm Sterling silver cable chain
- 10 3mm Swarovski bicone crystals, black
- 4 3mm Swarovski bicone crystals, clear
- 8 8mm Round Swarovski crystals, black/clear
- 2 6mm Swarovski bicone crystals, clear
- 4 4-5mm Faceted rock crystal cones
- 2 8-10mm Faceted rock crystal cones
- Pair of sterling earring findings with a loop
- **Tools:** Round- and chainnose pliers, diagonal wire cutters; hammer and anvil, optional

diameter slightly greater than that of the bead (**photo a**).

5 Swoop back to the other side of the top spiral and make another bend, as shown on the template.

6 Bend the wire back just past the center and make a small bend.

7 End the piece with a centering curve and a loop. Shape the piece as you want it to look. If desired, hammer it on both sides (use a ball peen hammer and a steel block or anvil).

8 Wrap a 3-in. (7.6cm) piece of fine gold-filled wire around the top, horizontal section of the wire 2-3 times, pressing the wraps together with chain-nose pliers (**photo b**). When you thread the pearl on the fine wire it will sit in the curve; move the first wrap to position the pearl correctly. Thread the pearl, cut the wire leaving about 1-2 in. (2.5-5cm), and wind it around the bottom of the swoop 2-3 times (**photo c**).

9 Attach a crystal between the outer edge of the spiral and the top of the bend on the other side. Then attach a

second large pearl in the large swoop on the other side of the earring.

10 Attach a crystal between the right and left swoops. Then attach the third crystal in the small, centered bend. Attach a small pearl or a fourth crystal in the centering curve above the loop.

11 Thread the third large pearl on a head pin and begin a ⅜-in. (1cm) wrapped loop (see "Basics," p. 136). Attach it to the loop at the bottom of the earring before completing the wrap.

12 Open the loop on the finding and attach it to the top of the spiral.

13 Make the second earring, preferably hanging it as a mirror image of the first.

chandelier earrings

1 Bend a 3-in. (7.6cm) piece of twist wire to match the full-size template (**figure 2**).

2 String a 3mm black crystal and a black and clear bead on a head pin and start a large wrapped loop. Hang the loop from the center loop on the twist wire and complete the wrap.

3 Start a medium-sized wrapped loop on the remains of the head pin and hook it to the top of the center loop on the twist wire before completing the wrap. String a black and clear bead and make a wrapped loop on the plane perpendicular to the first loop.

4 Cut a length of chain with an odd number of links (23-25) that is long enough to hang between the loops at the ends of the twist wire and curve below the center bead. Open each loop sideways to attach the end links of the chain (see "Basics"). Close the loops tightly.

5 Make two side dangles: On a head pin string a 3mm black crystal, a black and clear bead, a small crystal cone, and a 3mm clear crystal. Start a wrapped loop that will have 3-5 wraps and attach it to a loop at the end of the twist wire outside the chain. Complete the wrap. Bend the head pins slightly so the dangles hang vertically.

6 For the center dangle, string a 3mm black crystal, a large crystal cone, a 6mm crystal, and a 3mm black crystal. Start a wrapped loop and hang it from the center chain link before wrapping.

7 Hang the chandelier from the loop on the earring and make the other earring. ●

a

b

c

figure 1

figure 2

Shimmer aplenty

String a multi-strand necklace with sleek appeal

by Pam O'Connor

There are those who subscribe to the edict "less is more" and those who believe that more is always better. Here's a necklace to please both camps: a sleek, sophisticated design that contains an abundance of beads. It looks expensive but is made with inexpensive supplies. The sparkling 9º 3-cut beads frame a section of matte, size 2 bugle beads on each strand. Their close correspondence in diameter gives the necklace a graceful drape. I made two variations on this theme. In the champagne and white necklace, the bugle beads are centered. In the blue and white necklace, I placed them off-center.

stepbystep

❶ Decide on the length of your necklace. I wanted mine to frame my neckline, but the design translates well to a longer length. Each of my strands is 18 in. (46cm), not including the clasp. The strands on the champagne necklace have 7 in. (18cm) of 3-cut beads, 4 in. (10cm) of bugle beads, and another

materials
- 2-3 Hanks 9º 3-cut beads
- 1 Hank size 2 bugle beads
- 8 Bead tips
- 1 Toggle or S-hook clasp
- 4-6 6mm Split rings
- Beading cord, #0, or Silamide
- Beading needles, #10
- Twisted wire beading needles
- G-S Hypo cement
- Tools: round- and chainnose pliers, awl

7 in. of 3-cuts. The blue necklace strands are strung with 5 in. (13cm) of 3-cut beads, 4 in. of bugle beads, and 9 in. (23cm) of 3-cut beads. Both necklaces have 24 strands.

❷ Cut 1½ yd. (1.4m) of beading cord and thread a needle. Center the needle on the cord so that your working strand is doubled. String a stop bead, leaving a 6-in. (15cm) tail. Go through the stop bead again in the same direction to secure it. String the 3-cut beads and bugle beads following the measurements in step 1 or your own design. String another stop bead and go through it again.

❸ Repeat step 2 five more times.

❹ Remove the stop beads from one end of the six finished strands. Knot all the strands together with a firm overhand knot (see "Basics," p. 136) on one end. Push the beads against the knot so that there are no thread gaps. Remove the stop beads at the other end of the strands and tie another overhand knot. Insert an awl into the knot before it tightens and use the awl to slide the knot tightly against the beads (**photo a**).

❺ Pull all the cord tails on each end into a bead tip with a twisted wire needle. Divide the tails in half and tie

a surgeon's knot (see "Basics") inside each bead tip (**photo b**). Glue these knots. When the glue is dry, clip the cord tails and close the bead tips with chainnose pliers.

❻ Repeat steps 2-5 three more times.

❼ Attach a chain of two or three split rings to the bar side of the toggle clasp so the bar will fold flat for fastening. Attach 1 split ring to the ring side. Attach 4 bead tips to the end split ring on each side with roundnose pliers. ●

Show it off

Stringing meant to be seen

by Louise Malcolm

Most bead stringing experts tell you that the cord is never supposed to show in a well-made piece. But "never" is a word that I always take as a challenge. I believe that every rule is made to be broken, as illustrated here. This necklace highlights a few large beads on an attractive cord. Knots on both sides of each bead cluster hold the groups in place on the cord. The openness keeps the necklace light and gives it an airy look that's just right for warm-weather fashions. A more formal version of the same approach would use pearls spaced out on silk and held apart with knots. However you apply it, this technique breaks another stringing rule in that you string on single cord, not double.

stepbystep

Choose an assortment of beads that look good together. Variation of size, shape, color, and texture is the key to a successful design. Go for a random look, but add subtle continuity by repeating a few similar bead groups. You'll also get a more harmonious look if you graduate bead sizes within each group.

I've made this necklace very long so I can wrap it several times. Another alternative is to make a multi-strand and join the ends in cones (see p. 43). In this case, make sure that the beads on the various strands hang at different places.

❶ Cut the cord the desired length of the necklace plus an extra yard (.9m) for knots. Tie a temporary bead near one end, leaving a 6-8-in. tail (15-20cm). Stiffen the other end by pulling it through beeswax 2-3 times to make threading the beads easier.

② Pick out a group of the largest-holed beads. These beads must accommodate 5 strands of cord. String this bead or group of beads, but do not knot on either side of it. You will make these two knots last when you join the strand invisibly.

③ Tie an overhand knot ½-1½ in. (1.3-3.8cm) past the large bead (see "Basics," p. 136 and **photo a**).

④ String on any bead or small group of beads and slide it/them against the knot. Tie another overhand knot against the last bead of the group. Begin and end bead groups with a seed bead or small-holed bead so the big beads won't slip over the knots.

⑤ Repeat steps 3 and 4, using an awl to position each knot snugly against the bead or bead group (see "awl knotting" at right).

materials

- **10-20** Large beads (ceramic beads by Dana Swisher set the theme for the necklace)
- **1** Large bead with a hole large enough to hold 5 strands of cord
- Variety of medium-sized beads, shells, and bone shapes
- Small beads and bone, horn, and wood rondelles
- 7g Seed beads, 6º or 8º
- 3 yd. (2.7m) Hemp or waxed linen cord
- Beeswax
- G-S Hypo cement or clear nail polish
- Tools: awl, twisted wire beading needles (optional)

⑥ Leave a cord tail of at least 6 in. (15cm) when you've knotted after the last bead group.

⑦ To finish the necklace, thread the 6-in. tail through the starting large-holed bead or group. You now have a continuous strand with the two cord ends going through the bead (or bead group) in opposite directions. There should be about 1½ in. of cord between this bead(s) and the first and last knotted beads. Tie the ending tail around the strand cord with 1-2 half-hitch knots (see "Basics") right against the bead (**photo b**). Seal the knot with glue if you are not using waxed cord.

⑧ Remove the temporary bead from the starting end and stiffen the end with beeswax. Tie it around the strand cord on the other side of the bead as in step 7 and glue the knot if necessary.

⑨ To protect the knots, thread each end back through the large-holed bead when the glue is dry (**photo c**) and clip them flush to the bead. You may need to use a twisted wire needle or a dental floss threader to help pull the cords through the now full bead hole. **•**

awl knotting

by Louise Malcolm

All pearl knotting techniques require practice, but using an awl is probably the easiest to master. For a necklace with knots between each bead, cut a cord four times the length of the finished necklace plus at least 12 in. (31cm) and string with doubled cord. (Cord is cheap; starting over is a pain.) Choose cord that fills the bead holes but can pass through the beads the required number of times. With bead tips, doubled cord goes through the beads once; with French wire, five passes are needed.

stepbystep

If you plan to begin and end the strand with a bead tip, see "Basics," p. 136. Tie your first knot against the bead tip. If you attach the clasp with French wire, as shown here, knot after the first bead and before the last one (see p. 64).

❶ After working the clasp attachment you prefer, string all the beads. Push them toward the needle and tie the cord loosely around the last bead.

❷ Push the first bead up to the clasp. Form an overhand knot by looping the cord around the first three fingers of your left hand.

❸ Drop the starting end through the loop between your fingers (**photo a**).

❹ Insert the awl in the loop from the starting end toward the needle end (**photo b**).

❺ Keeping the awl in the loop, pull the cord to the left away from the awl. As you pull, the loop will tighten and slide toward the bead and the tip of the awl (**photo c**).

Use your thumb and index fingernails to push the knot tight against the bead or bead tip as it slips onto the tip of the awl and then off (**photo d**).

❻ Separate the cords and pull them apart to seat the knot tight against the bead (**photo e**). If you pull too hard, the cord will tear.

❼ Push up the next bead and repeat the process until you've knotted the last bead. **•**

Classic
multi-strand bracelets

Use toggles, braids, and hidden knots to enhance a basic design

by Nicolette Stessin

a

Bracelets are subject to more abuse and stress than any other piece of jewelry. After all, your hands and wrists are constantly moving and in contact with hard surfaces. So bracelets need to be constructed to have extra strength, which means stringing your beads with doubled thread whenever possible. When it comes to choosing the right clasp, consider spring rings, lobster claws, magnetic clasps, and toggles; but keep in mind that the first two can be hard to fasten by yourself.

b

stepbystep

These multi-strand bracelets demonstrate several versatile finishing techniques, including chain and beaded toggle leads, a two-bead method for hiding knots, and a braiding option.

six-strand bracelets
Make the blue tiny-tears bracelet and the silver and white version using these basic stringing and finishing techniques.

❶ Cut six 1-yd. (.9m) lengths of #1 beading cord. Thread the cords through the loop on the clasp's ring end, center the clasp, and tie the cords together with an overhand knot (see "Basics," p. 136) (**photo a**).

Before gluing the knot, make sure that it is not too bulky to fit through the hole in your 6mm bead. If it is, try dividing the cords into two groups. Make an overhand knot with each group of cords and position one knot slightly above the other.

❷ String all 12 cords through a 6mm bead to hide the overhand knot or knots. (Add a second silver bead, if desired, as shown in the silver and white bracelet.) Thread a twisted wire needle onto a pair of cords and string about 6½ in. (16.3cm) of beads. String the other 5 strands to match.

Once the beads are strung, check

how comfortably the bracelet fits around your wrist and add or remove beads as necessary. The bracelet should drape softly below your wrist bone.

❸ String all 12 cord ends through another 6mm silver bead. Pull 8 cords to the side and string the remaining 4 through at least three 6º or 8º beads to make the toggle lead. Go through the loop on the toggle's bar end and back through the seed beads (**photo b**).

For the silver and white bracelet, string a silver bead on the 4 cords that you'll use for the toggle lead. Then string at least 3 seed beads to make the lead. Go through the loop and back through the seed beads. Continue through the second silver bead added in step 3.

❹ Tighten the cords, making sure that no thread shows. Tie the 4-cord group and the 8-cord group together with the first half of a square knot (**photo c**). Test the length again.

❺ When the bracelet length is right, tie the strands together with a surgeon's knot (see "Basics"), glue the knot thoroughly, and let dry. Use a twisted wire needle to help work the cord ends through the large bead (it will take several passes to get all the cords through the bead) and pull the cords gently to ease the knot into the bead. Trim the ends close to the large bead.

c

materials
- Small toggle clasp
- Twisted wire beading needles
- G-S Hypo cement

tiny-tears bracelet
- 42 in. (1.1m) Tiny-teardrop beads (small drops with top holes)
- 4-5 6º or 8º Seed beads
- 2 6mm Large-holed silver beads
- Nylon beading cord, #1

white and silver bracelet
- 40 in. (1m) 8º Seed beads, matte finish, silver-lined, clear
- 72 2.5mm Square Bali silver spacer beads
- 4 6mm Large-holed silver beads
- Nylon beading cord, #1

gemstone bracelet
- 2 20 in. (51cm) Strands 6-8mm faceted semi-precious stones
- 5 4mm Silver split rings
- 2 6mm Large-holed silver beads
- 2 4mm Silver beads
- Nylon beading cord, #3

toggles: the perfect clasp

Toggles have been around for a long time, and a wide variety of styles and sizes are readily available. The design is clean and efficient. But best of all, they're so easy to use that most people can fasten a toggle bracelet without help.

A toggle consists of two parts: a ring and a bar, as shown in **figure 2**. The toggle bar must be equipped with a lead, a short chain or strand of seed beads that's just over half the length of the toggle bar, in order to insert and remove it from the ring. Furthermore, the width of the bar and lead together must be a bit narrower than the opening of the toggle ring (**figure 3**).

Remember the bracelet's need for strength? The lead is the part of a bracelet that takes the greatest stress. If it's made of chain, the links must be soldered. And if you have to attach your own chain lead, do so with small split rings used in parallel as though they were one. Never attach the lead with a jump ring.

figure 2

figure 3

three-strand bracelet

❶ Cut one 1-yd. (.9m) and one 24-in. (60cm) length of #3 beading cord. (You don't need to double a cord of this thickness.) Thread the longer cord through the loop on the toggle clasp's ring end and center it. Thread the 24-in. length through the same loop. Position this cord so that one tail is about 18-in. (45cm) long. String a 4mm silver bead onto all four cords.

❷ Tie the 4 cords with an overhand knot just below the silver bead and glue the knot. String a 6mm silver bead on

the 4 cord ends to hide the knot (**photo d**). You now have three 18-in. lengths of cord and a 6-in. (15cm) length coming out of the large bead.

❸ String about 6½ in. of gemstones on the three longer cords. Take the short tail through the first 2-3 beads on any of the strands and trim it. Check the bracelet's fit and add or remove beads as necessary.

❹ Make a short chain lead on the toggle bar by linking 2 pairs of split rings. Connect the chain to the toggle with a single split ring (**photo e**).

❺ String a 6mm silver bead onto the 3 beaded cords. Pull 2 cords to the side, and string a 4mm bead on the remaining cord. Loop that cord around the end pair of split rings attached to the toggle bar and go back through the 4mm bead (**photo e**).

❻ Tie the strands together using a surgeon's knot and glue it securely. Work the cords through the larger bead and pull the ends gently until the knot is hidden. Trim the ends.

easy braiding technique

The following braid is easiest to do with a 3-strand bracelet or necklace, but it also works on a 6-strand piece as long as you're using smaller beads. Use the technique when you want to change the look of your multi-strand jewelry.

It's important to experiment with the braid before you finish your bracelet. You may have to adjust its length if the braiding shortens it too much. The silver and white bracelet, for example, becomes almost an inch (2.5cm) shorter after braiding. Pieces made with larger beads shrink even more.

❶ Think about the space between the outer and center strands as bays (**figure 1**). Fold down the toggle ring and put it through bay 1 from the front (**photo f**).

❷ Now come around the back and go through bay 2 from the front (**photo g**).

❸ Repeat these two steps until the braided bracelet is firm but not stiff. Untwist the bracelet by reversing the steps and going through the bays in the opposite direction. ●

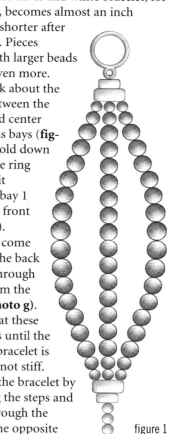

figure 1

Cause a stir

Jointed dangles give these earrings motion

by Pam O'Connor

Put a little swing in your step with these sensational jointed earrings. A single joint gives the gold Chinese lantern earrings (right) a bit of swish, while the multiple joints of the geometric earrings (below) will add a twinkle to your every gesture.

Bead caps in graduated sizes are the secret to making the Chinese lantern earrings. Use bicone crystals to separate the caps and simulate the glitter of a lit lantern.

I found the assortment of charms for the geometric earrings in a mail order catalog. The simple, handwrought shapes provide a sleek, modern look. The charms are connected with simple wire loop and bead joints.

a   b

c

d

stepbystep

geometric earrings

❶ Snip the head off a head pin and make a loop at the bottom of the pin (see "Basics," p. 136). String a 3mm silver bead. Trim the remaining wire to ⅜ in. (1cm) and make a loop. Turn the loop in the same direction as the first loop, so the wire ends close on the same side and the loops are in the same plane (**photo a**).

❷ Open a loop to the side and attach it to the square earring finding, entering from the front. Close the loop. Connect the other loop to the gold circle charm in the same manner (**photo b**).

❸ Repeat step 1, stringing a 3mm gold bead on the wire.

❹ Attach one loop to the bottom of the circle charm and the other end to the silver square charm as in step 2.

❺ String a 4mm gold bead on a head pin. Trim the wire above the bead to ⅜ in. and make a loop. Attach the loop to the square charm's bottom hole, entering from the front.

❻ Repeat steps 1-5 to make the second earring.

Chinese lantern earrings

❶ Place a crystal, a 6mm bead cap, a crystal, an 8mm bead cap, a crystal, and a 10mm bead cap on a head pin (**photo c**).

❷ Make a wrapped loop above the largest bead cap (see "Basics"). These earring findings have a 3mm space between the loop for hanging a dangle and the bottom edge of the decorative disk on the finding. To compensate for the gap, I made four wraps on each loop so that the top bead cap would swing clear of the earring finding.

materials

geometric earrings
- **2** 8mm Square post-earring findings, sterling silver
- **2** 9mm Square charms, sterling silver
- **2** 12mm Circle charms, vermeil
- **6** Head pins, sterling silver
- **2** 3mm Beads, sterling silver
- **2** 3mm Beads, gold-filled
- **2** 4mm Beads, gold-filled

Chinese lantern earrings
- **2** Decorative earring wires with hidden loops, vermeil
- **2** 6mm Bead caps, vermeil
- **2** 8mm Bead caps, vermeil
- **2** 10mm Bead caps, vermeil
- **6** 4mm Bicone crystals,
- **2** Head pins, gold-filled
(all findings available from Rishashay, 800-517-3311)
- Tools: Round- and chainnose pliers, diagonal wire cutters

❸ Open the hook closure on the earring finding slightly to allow the dangle to be attached. Slide the wrapped loop into place on the earring finding (**photo d**) and close the hook.

❹ Repeat steps 1-3 to make the second earring. ●

Making odd ends meet

A beautiful, random-patterned neck-lace is not the result of haphazard stringing. In fact, successful random designs take special planning. To achieve balance within a random pattern, you must consider the color, size, weight, shape, and texture of the beads. Here are some design guidelines.

choosing your beads

Start with color. Lay out several color combinations from your bead stash and go with what catches your eye first. If your bead stock is too limited to offer inspiration, visit a bead store or even a fabric store to seek appealing color combinations. You can also peruse art books and magazines. Wonderful color palettes may be found everywhere if you train your eye to see them.

I love the mysterious quality a piece of jewelry acquires from a mix of ethnic beads and charms. For the necklace shown here, I selected the spotted black beads as a starting point. I chose black seed beads to set off the bright red, blue, and green accent beads I chose to coor-dinate with the dots on the focal beads.

I think seed beads are the best way to separate the larger beads, providing space for each one to make a statement. I couldn't resist the faux Phoenician head bead, the many-colored eye beads, the brass hand and face charms, and a few Chinese clear-glass beads with images painted inside.

When selecting the rest of the beads, I looked for different sizes, shapes, and textures within my color palette. If all the beads are shiny or matte, they lose differentiation and visual impact. In other projects, my bead choices have run the gamut from semi-precious stones and crystals to wood, metal, and artisan glass beads. I believe variety makes for a more interesting necklace—

Unite a bead miscellany in a cone-capped necklace

by Adele Clausen

as long as you adhere to a color palette and follow the few design provisions outlined below.

arranging your beads

After you decide on the length of your necklace (see step 1 below), lay out your accent beads on a necklace design board or other work surface. Start with the largest beads and space them apart on all three strands as a group and on each individual strand.

Heavy beads, such as the Phoenician head bead, need to be balanced by another heavy bead or a combination of beads on the opposite side of the strand. Also, position the larger beads toward the middle of a strand so they take center stage in your design and the weight is centered.

Because the first 3-4 in. (7.5-10cm) on each side will be around the back of your neck, use smaller beads than in the strands' centers. As you position the rest of the accent beads, vary color and texture as well as size.

Group two or three beads into small clusters and cap large-hole beads with smaller ones so the seed beads don't slide into the hole. There is no need to position the seed beads on your design board, but you might scatter small silver spacer beads throughout the strands to add another unifying element.

stepbystep

❶ Determine your necklace's length. The short strand on my necklace is 20 in. (51cm) long. The middle and long strands are 23 and 26 in. (58 and 66cm), respectively.
❷ Plan your design as described above.
❸ Cut 1½ yd. (1.4m) of cord and thread a needle to the center, doubling the cord. String a stop bead 6 in. (15cm)

from the tail and sew back through it in the same direction to secure it.
❹ String 1½-2 in. (3.8-5cm) of seed beads before stringing the first small accent bead on the short strand. Vary the number of seed beads between each accent bead or group of accent beads, gauging the strand length as you string. When you have strung the last accent bead, you should need another 1½-2 in. of seed beads to reach 20 in. String another stop bead and go through it again in the same direction.
❺ Repeat steps 3-4 for the middle and long strands, starting with 5 ft. and 2 yd. (1.5 and 1.8m) of bead cord, respectively.
❻ Remove the stop beads on one end of all three strands. Tie the tails together in an overhand knot (see "Basics," p. 136). Remove the stop beads from the other end of the strands. Push the beads up so they are flush against the knot at the other end and there is no slack. Tie the tails into another overhand knot, using an awl to tighten the knot against the beads (see "Basics").
❼ Cut 2 in. (5cm) of wire, positioning the wire cutters with the flat side toward the 2-in. piece of wire.
❽ Make an eye or loop with the last ⅜ in. (1cm) of wire (see "Basics").
❾ Thread half the tail ends through the eye in each direction (**photo a**). Tie them to the eye with a couple of surgeon's knots (see "Basics") and glue the knot. When the glue is dry, trim the tails to ¼ in. (6mm).
❿ Pull the wire end through the cone from the wide end (**photo b**). Cut off all but ⅜ in. of the wire (**photo c**). Make another eye or loop as in step 8.
⓫ Repeat steps 7-10 on the necklace's other side.
⓬ Attach a split ring to each loop and connect them with a large S-hook (**photo d**). ●

a

b

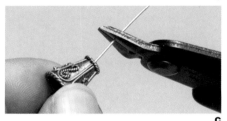

c

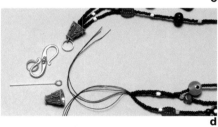

d

materials

- **75-100** Assorted accent beads and charms
- **1** Hank 11º seed beads
- **4-6 in.** (10-15cm) 18-Gauge wire, half-hard
- **2** Cones
- **1** S-hook clasp
- **2** 5mm Split rings
- Nylon beading cord, #1 or 3
- Beading needles, #10 or twisted wire needles
- G-S Hypo cement
- Tools: chain- and roundnose pliers, diagonal wire cutters

What to do with leftover beads

Head pins turn mixed pearls into fine jewelry

by Nancy Alden

Like me, you probably have little boxes and tubes with six pink pearls left over from that necklace, four gray ones from another piece, a dozen mauve ones from still another project, and on and on. Then, of course, there are all the leftover spacers, bead caps, and semi-precious stones—all small and all much too good to waste. If you've been making jewelry for a while, you probably won't need to buy a thing to make your version of my leftover pearls necklace, but you may want to add a few stones or some new vermeil spacers. (Bead shopping is always fun.)

stepbystep

My 16-in. (41cm) necklace has 67 dangles, but the number of dangles on your necklace may be different, either because you change the length or because the pearls on your necklace strand are a different size. When you string the necklace, alternate a pearl and a dangle, beginning and ending with a pearl. It's important that you use thin or ultra-thin head pins; standard head pins won't fit through the pearls.

❶ Decide on the length you want the finished necklace to be and subtract 1 in. (2.5cm) for the clasp. Start by making about 10 dangles of varying lengths. To make a dangle, string a pleasing arrangement of beads (spacers, bead caps, gold beads, stone beads, or stone rondelles) and pearls on a head pin. (See the photo to get ideas for your dangles.) They should vary in length from ⅜-¹³⁄₁₆ in. (1-2cm), including the loop. Make a medium-sized wrapped loop above the beads, leaving enough space for 1-5 wraps (see "Basics," p. 136). The number of wraps should vary.

❷ String the dangles alternately with round pearls (mine are 4.5-5mm). Measure to determine how many pearls and dangles occupy an inch. You will need about 15 times this number of pearls and dangles. Now make the number of dangles you'll need.

❸ Arrange your dangles in a pleasing order, staggering them so the large beads are at different levels.

❹ To string the necklace, start with a 24-in. (61cm) length of flexible beading wire. On one end, string a flat spacer, a 3mm gold bead, a crimp bead, and one end of the clasp. Leave everything at this end of the wire. Bring a 2-3-in. (5-8cm) tail of wire back through the crimp, the gold bead, and the spacer (**figure**), and use crimping pliers (or chainnose pliers) to crimp the crimp bead tightly. Cut the short tail off flush with the spacer bead. Now alternately string a pearl then a dangle until the

necklace is 15½ in. (39cm) long, counting the first half of the clasp.

❺ End with a pearl. String a spacer, a 3mm gold bead, a crimp bead, and the other half of the clasp. Bring the tail back through the crimp, the gold bead, and the spacer. Tighten the beads, leaving just enough ease to allow the necklace to hang gracefully, and crimp the crimp bead. Cut off the tail of wire flush with the spacer. ●

materials

- 1 16-in. (40cm) Strand 4.5-5mm nearly round freshwater pearls (approx. 68)
- 24 in. (61cm) Flexible beading wire, .014
- 2 Crimp beads
- 2 3mm Beads
- 1 Spring ring clasp with a soldered jump ring, gold filled
- Dangle supplies:
  - 67 (approx.) thin head pins
  - **50-60** 2-2.5mm Beads
  - **50-60** 4mm Spacers
  - **6-10** 4-5mm Beads and bead caps
  - **15-20** 4.5mm Bead caps
  - **50-75** 2-8mm Assorted pearls
  - **50-60** 2-4mm Assorted semi-precious stone beads (garnet, iolite, moonstone, quartz, tourmaline, etc.)
  - **40-50** 3-5mm Assorted semi-precious stone rondelles
- Tools: roundnose, chainnose, and crimping pliers; diagonal wire cutters

String a vintage look

Tassel pendants add a retro touch

by Deb Gottlieb

I am a fan of the past. I love 1950s floral prints, the long vests that Mary Tyler Moore wore over high-waisted trousers, and anything Art Deco. I haunt antiques stores, flea markets, and rummage sales to find old jewelry, vintage clothing, buttons, hats, and beads. Some of my best finds have been made searching through what looked like real junk. And my favorite pieces are always the ones with tassels.

Recently, I've been drawn to jewelry from the 1920s and '30s, so I designed a pair of necklaces to reflect those vintage styles. And, of course, each one features a tassel.

stepbystep

To recreate this vintage look, design a necklace that is at least 30 in. (75cm) long and choose a tassel style that complements it. Two versions are shown here, but you can choose among many tassel variations. (See Valerie Campbell-Harding's book, *Beaded Tassels, Braids & Fringes*, Sterling Publishing, 1999, for inspiration.) You can assemble these necklaces in one of two ways: either design and string the entire necklace and then attach the tassel, or string the tassel when you reach the necklace's midpoint. As always, when you string beads for jewelry, work on doubled cord.

beaded tassel
❶ Select a bead for the tassel head. (I chose a bead with a ½ in. (1.3cm) diameter and a

---

materials

both necklaces
- Nylon beading cord, #1 or Silamide
- Beading needles, #10 or twisted wire beading needles
- Clear nail polish
- Clasp
- Tools: Round- and chain-nose pliers, wire cutters

blue and yellow necklace
- Mix of Czech glass beads and fire-polished crystals
- Head pin or 3 in. (7.6cm) medium-gauge half-hard wire
- Small amount of seed beads

pearl and carnelian necklace
- 16-in. (41cm) Strand fresh-water pearls
- 16-in. Strand faceted carnelian beads
- 12 yd. (11m) Silk or rayon cord
- 3-in. Chain
- 2 Split rings
- Tatool tassel frame or cardboard

a

b

c

good-sized hole.) Make a wrapped loop (see "Basics," p. 136) on the head pin and cut off the head. The loop must be small enough to fit into the bead's hole.

❷ Thread a needle with 2 yd. (1.8m) of cord and tie the tails onto the loop.

❸ String 3-4 in. (7.6-10cm) of beads and a seed bead to make the first tassel strand. Turn, skip the seed bead, and go back through the beads to the wire loop. Sew through the loop and back through the first bead on the strand (**photo a**).

❹ Continue making strands until you reach the tassel's desired fullness. Tie the cord to the loop, glue the knots, and trim the threads.

❺ Pull the straight end of the head pin through the tassel head. Add a few more beads to the head pin, if desired (**photo b**).

❻ Make the first half of a wrapped loop close to the last bead strung on the head pin. Make the loop large enough to keep it from being pulled back through the bead.

❼ If you've already strung your necklace, attach the tassel before you complete the wraps (**photo c**). Otherwise, finish the wrapped loop and string the tassel when you string the necklace.

fiber tassel

❶ Determine the finished length of the tassel. Cut a small rectangle of cardboard to that size or adjust the tassel frame.

❷ Tape one end of the cord to the frame. Keeping the tension even, wrap about 10 yd. (9m) of cord around the frame to make the skirt (**photo d**). Cut the cord, leaving a 1-yard (.9m) tail.

❸ Pinch the tops of the wrapped cords together and pull a 1-ft. (30cm) piece of beading cord through them. Tie this cord to secure the tassel skirt temporarily (**photo e**).

❹ Ease the skirt off the frame and keep the loops parallel. Fold the shorter of the two cord ends into a 2-in. (5cm) U-shape and lay it next to the skirt. Bring the cut end up so it extends past the tassel's top.

❺ Wrap the cord's long end neatly around the top of the tassel and thread it through the U made in step 4 (**photo f**). Pull gently on the U's cut end to coax the long cord inside the wraps to secure it. Trim both cord ends close to the tassel.

❻ Cut through the skirt loops and trim the bottom edge so the ends are even.

❼ Use the beading cord gathering the wraps to pull the chain through the tassel as follows: Cut the cord at the knot and tie one end to

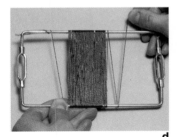

d

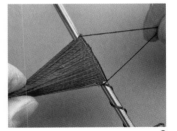

e

f

g

the last link in the chain. Carefully pull the chain through the top of the tassel. Cut the cord off the chain.

❽ Remove links to shorten the chain, if necessary, and attach the last link on each side to a split ring (**photo g**).

Connect this split ring to another one so the tassel will face forward. If you've already strung your necklace, slide the top split ring around the beading cord. Or string the tassel as you string the necklace. ◉

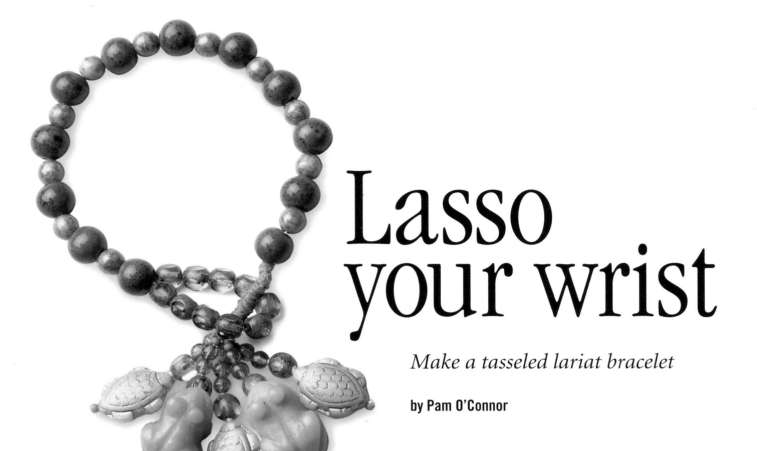

Lasso your wrist

Make a tasseled lariat bracelet

by Pam O'Connor

The unexpected inspiration for this lariat bracelet was a friend with the noisy habit of wearing her keychain around her wrist. We laughed about her "bracelet," and then I felt the exhilarating tingle of an idea. "Why not lariat bracelets?" I thought. Applying the lariat concept to the wrist posed a design challenge. How can you get it over your hand and onto your wrist to stay? The design solution is a beaded tassel. The gradual increase in bead size on each fringe prevents the loop from sliding over the tassel but allows the bracelet to widen enough to slide your hand through. The weight of the tassel then tethers the bracelet securely.

materials

- Nylon beading cord, #3
- Twisted wire beading needles
- Waxed linen in coordinating color
- G-S Hypo cement

frog and turtle bracelet
- **12** 8mm Ceramic beads
- **11** 6mm Glass beads
- **15** 6mm Pressed-glass beads
- **15** 11º Seed beads
- **2** Frog charms
- **3** Turtle beads

pearl and crystal bracelet
- **16** 6x10mm Glass rondelle beads
- **21** 6mm Czech fire-polished crystals
- **31** 4mm Czech fire-polished crystals
- **6** 6x10mm Freshwater pearls
- **6** 12x8mm Rose quartz lozenge beads
- **6** 11º Seed beads

step by step

Fold your hand with the thumb and little finger touching as you would to slide on a bangle bracelet and measure its widest circumference. Your bracelet must widen to this length plus ¼ in. (6mm). This calculates to 8½ in. (22cm) for my hand. My bracelets have a 7 in. (18cm) beaded length with a 1½ in. (4cm) loop of beads at one end. The 1½-in. tassel is lashed to the other end with a 1-in.-long (2.5cm) waxed linen wrap.

❶ Cut a 30-in. (76cm) length of beading cord. String 1½ in. of 4-6mm beads. Move the beads to the center of the cord and string both cord ends through a larger bead to begin the main section of the bracelet (**photo a**).

❷ String 7 in. of larger beads (7-10mm) over both cords. If you alternate bead sizes, start and end with the larger bead. Tie a square knot (see "Basics," p. 136) against the last bead to keep the beaded length snug.

❸ Cut two 12-in. (31cm) lengths of cord. With their ends even, tie them together in the middle with an overhand

knot (see "Basics"). Fold the knotted cords in half at the knot to make 4 ends. Place the knotted cords alongside the cord ends of the bracelet with the knot close to the last bead. These strands will become the tassel.

❹ To lash the cords together, cut an 18-in. (46cm) length of waxed linen and fold over 4 in. (10cm) to create a loop at one end. Place the loop toward the cord ends and extend about 1 in. of the loop's tail toward the bead loop, overlapping the bracelet. Leave this end unlashed and begin wrapping the long end of the waxed linen around all the cords, pushing the first wraps tightly against the beads (**photo b**). Lash firmly and evenly to cover the overhand knot and secure it to the bracelet (**photo c**).

❺ After you have lashed 1 in., cut the remaining linen cord to 3 in. (7.5cm) and thread all 3 in. through the loop (**photo d**). Pull the cord tail at the start of the lashing to bring the loop and cord end under the lashing. Trim the tails.

❻ Before you string the tassel, put the fringe cords through the bracelet loop. Thread a twisted wire needle on a cord end and string each fringe as specified. Each frog and turtle fringe contains two 11º seed beads, two 4mm glass beads, one 6mm glass bead, a frog or turtle charm, and an 11º seed bead. I trimmed off the sixth fringe cord for the frog and turtle bracelet at the edge of the lashing. Five charmed fringes was substantial enough for the design. Each of the six pearl tassel fringes contains two 4mm fire-polished crystals, one 6mm fire-polished crystal, 1 freshwater pearl, 1 rose quartz bead, one 4mm fire-polished crystal, and an 11º seed bead. To end a fringe, skip the last 11º seed bead and go back through the next bead (**photo e**). Tie a double half-hitch knot (see "Basics") and go up one bead. Tie another double half-hitch knot, go through another bead or two, and clip the tail end. Secure the knots with a drop of glue. ◗

a

b

c

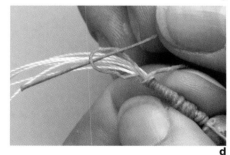

d

e

Graceful geometrics

*String elegant jewelry with cross-needle
weaving's building-block technique*

by May Frank

Cross-needle weaving is a versatile bead-stringing technique using pairs of needles. You string a bead or beads on each needle, then bring both needles through a center bead from opposite directions. The threads cross inside the center bead to complete the stitch.

materials

all pieces shown
- Metallic or nylon beading thread to match main bead color and size
- Twisted wire needles
- Bead tips
- G-S Hypo cement or clear nail polish
- Tools: Round- and chainnose pliers

lapis lazuli and crystal necklace
- 2 16-in. (41cm) Strands 4mm lapis beads
- 1 16-in. Strand 6mm lapis beads
- 1 50-Bead strand 4mm Czech fire-polished crystals
- 1 4mm Split ring
- 1 6mm Split ring
- Lobster claw clasp

gold bead and pearl necklace
- 200 4mm Czech beads, rose-gold
- 1 16-in. Strand 2mm pearls
- Magnetic clasp

garnet and crystal bracelet
- 1 16-in. Strand 6mm bicone garnets
- 50 4mm Czech fire-polished crystals
- Magnetic clasp

The basic technique makes a beaded strip consisting of two outside edges and a center row. You can vary the look by changing bead shapes, quantities, sizes, and color placement. The two very different necklaces shown at right were made using exactly the same technique. To increase the width, simply add rows, as in the bracelet shown on page 54.

stepbystep

When you work in cross-needle weave, be careful not to pierce a thread with a needle as you cross inside a bead. Generally, the best way to avoid this is to cross both needles through the center bead at the same time. If the holes in your beads are too small to accommodate two needles at once, work with the dullest needles you have available or use twisted wire needles, as I do.

To keep the thread from abrading as you work on a long piece such as a necklace, start the stitches in the center, using the technique described below.

lapis and crystal necklace

This necklace look best in a 16-18 in. (41-46cm) length. Using large and small beads for the zigzag design creates a gentle arc that sits gracefully along the neckline.

❶ Cut a piece of beading cord at least four times the desired length of your necklace and thread it through a twisted wire needle. Center the needle on the cord and fold the cord in half. On doubled cord, string a bead halfway between the cut ends and the needle end to use as a stop bead, and take the thread through the bead once more in the same direction. Wrap the tail ends around a small piece of cardboard while you work with the needle end. Tape the cardboard to your work surface so both hands are free.

❷ Slide the needle out of the way and cut the cord in half at the fold. Thread a twisted wire needle onto the cord without one, so you'll be working with a right-hand and a left-hand needle.

❸ String two crystal beads on the right-hand needle, sliding the first onto the cord and leaving the second on the needle. String a 4mm bead on the left-hand needle and slide it onto the cord. Take the left-hand needle through the crystal on the right-hand needle, so the two needles cross inside the bead, as shown in **figure 1**. Pull the cords in opposite directions to tighten the stitch and slide the beads toward the stop bead.

❹ String two crystals on the left-hand needle, sliding the first onto the cord and leaving the second on the needle as in step 3. String a 6mm bead on the right-hand needle and slide it onto the

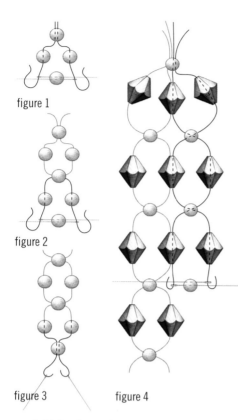

figure 1

figure 2

figure 3   figure 4

cord. Take the right-hand needle through the crystal on the left-hand needle so the needles cross inside the bead, and tighten the stitch (**figure 2**).

❺ Continue stringing crystals, alternating between 4mm and 6mm beads as described in steps 3 and 4 until you complete half the pattern, about 2¾ in. (7cm). Remember, you started in the center of the necklace.

❻ Continue working in cross-needle weave using 4mm beads until you reach the desired length for one side of the necklace. String both cords in the same direction through a 6mm bead (**figure 3**). Clamp or tape the ends temporarily while you work on the other side.

❼ Unwind the reserved cord and remove the stop bead. String the second half of the necklace to match the first.

❽ Hold the necklace around your neck

to check its length and add or remove beads from both sides equally. String a bead tip and a seed bead onto the pair of cords on each end of the necklace and make several surgeon's knots (see "Basics," p. 136) inside the bead tip. Glue the knots, trim the cord ends, and close the bead tip with chainnose pliers.

❾ To attach a lobster claw clasp, attach a 4mm split ring to one bead tip and a 6mm split ring to the other using roundnose pliers. Then attach the clasp to the smaller split ring.

gold bead and pearl necklace

❶ Start this necklace following the directions in steps 1-2 for the lapis necklace.

❷ String a gold bead and a pearl on the right-hand needle, sliding the gold bead onto the cord. String a gold bead on the left-hand needle and slide it onto the cord. Take the left-hand needle through the pearl, so the two needles cross inside it (**figure 1**). Pull the cords in opposite directions to tighten the stitch and slide the beads toward the stop bead. (If the pearl's hole is too small for both needles to pass through at one time, slide the pearl onto the cord before going through it with the other needle.)

❸ Continue to work in cross-needle weave (**figure 2**) until you reach the desired length for one side of the necklace. String both cords in the same direction through a pearl (**figure 3**). Clamp or tape the ends temporarily while you work on the other side.

❹ Follow the directions in steps 7-8, above, to complete the other half of the necklace.

❺ Attach each half of a magnetic clasp to a bead tip using roundnose pliers.

garnet and crystal bracelet

❶ Measure your wrist and add about ¾ in. (2cm) of ease. Since most clasps

plus bead tips will add about ¾ in. to a bracelet, make the beaded section the same as your wrist measurement.

❷ Cut 2 lengths of beading cord about four times the bracelet's finished length. Thread a twisted wire needle on each cord and knot the tails together about 4 in. (10cm) from the cut ends. Thread both needles through a bead tip and a crystal. Make a bulky overhand knot in the bead tip, glue the knot, and trim the cords. Close the bead tip with chainnose pliers.

❸ Set aside the needle and cord on the right-hand side. Cut the other cord at the fold and thread a twisted wire needle onto the half without one.

❹ String a garnet and a crystal onto the right-hand needle, sliding the garnet onto the cord. String a garnet onto the left-hand needle and slide it onto the cord. Take the left-hand needle through the crystal (**figure 2**) and pull the cords apart to tighten the stitch.

❺ Repeat step 4 until you've reached the length of your wrist measurement. Clamp or tape the cords while you add the next vertical row.

❻ Using the needle and cord that you set aside in step 3, cut the cord at the fold and thread a twisted wire needle onto the half without one.

❼ Thread the left-hand needle through the uppermost garnet on the right side of the strand you just completed. String a garnet and crystal on the right-hand needle. Take the left-hand needle through the crystal to make the stitch (**figure 4**). Repeat until you reach the end of the existing strand.

❽ String all four cords in the same direction through a crystal and a bead tip. Tie a bulky surgeon's knot, dab the knot with glue, trim the tails, and close the bead tip. Use roundnose pliers to attach each half of a magnetic clasp to the bead tips. ●

Charmed, I'm sure

Use charms and crystals for special earrings

by Alice Korach

W hen I go to the bead store, I always come home with more than I expected. Good examples of an impulse buy are the charms that form the base of my butterfly earrings (second from right).

In fact, any charm with multiple piercings around the edge is a great candidate for earrings, as shown above. You can attach dangles with plain loops, but wrapped loops are more secure and add a slightly decorative, designer touch.

stepbystep

❶ For the butterfly earrings, make 6 tiny rings of wire around the tip of your roundnose pliers for spacers on each dangle (**detail photo**). Cut flush and refine the shape on your pliers. (You can use these spacers in many projects.) Close them with chainnose pliers.

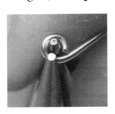

❷ Cut six 2-in. (5cm) lengths of wire for the dangles. To create the heads of head pins, make a tiny loop on one end of each. Squeeze the loop together side to side so it looks like a tiny paddle (see the bottoms of the dangles on the finished earring).

❸ For the first side dangle, string a pearl, a ring spacer, and a gold crystal on one wire.

❹ Begin a large wrapped loop (see "Basics," p. 136) above the crystal through step 3. Attach the loop to one of the bottom side holes on the charm and complete the wrap.

❺ For the middle dangle, string a gold crystal, a spacer, and a 7mm crystal. Attach it to the middle hole of the charm as in step 4.

❻ Make another side dangle as in steps 3 through 4.

❼ Since the butterfly doesn't have a centered top hole, attach two oval jump rings to the two top holes on the charm and then to the earring loop with the chainnose pliers. Open and close a jump

materials

butterfly earrings
- **2** Charms with multiple edge piercings (at least 3 on the bottom and 1 on top)
- **4** 5mm Pearls, bronze
- **6** 4mm Bicone crystals, gold
- **2** 7mm Bicone crystals, amber A/B
- **18** in. (46cm) 22-gauge Gold-filled wire, half-hard
- **4** 6.5x5mm Gold-filled oval jump rings
- Pair of post earrings with loop
- Tools: round- and chainnose pliers; diagonal wire cutter

ring sideways (don't pull it apart—see "Basics"). ●

On the Celtic knot earrings at left, Alice used 3mm Czech glass cubes, bronze glass 3-cut seed beads, and 2.5mm pearls. The silver-colored peweter Celtic knots feature Chinese crystals and 2mm and 4mm silver beads. The two-part antique gold pewter earrings at right combine 3 x 5mm Czech metallic glass bicone crystals, 10mm gray drop pearls and 13mm white oblong, knobby pearls.

Chained elegance

Create a tiered crystal necklace with chain spacers

by Alice Korach

Chain isn't just for hanging a pendant anymore. Many designers have begun using it as a spacing element in complex bead jewelry. And in this elaborate-looking design, it also serves to increase the depth of the front of the necklace. If you're making a necklace with only two bands of chain and beads above, below, and between the chains, all the beads can be the same size, but when you add additional chains to deepen the necklace, you also have to increase bead size and skip links to allow the necklace to flare so it will fit properly.

step by step

After cutting the chain pieces, string the beads from the center out, alternating sides. If you're using wire instead of head pins, cut 3-in. (7.6cm) pieces and make a tiny loop at the top to serve as a head. Before attaching the clasp, check the necklace for length.

The pearls I used for dangles are expensive. You can substitute glass dangles, hanging top-drilled dangle beads as shown on p. 16.

❶ Cut two 17-in. (43cm) lengths of chain, one 11-in. (28cm) length, and one 9-in. (23cm) length.

❷ String 1 MC crystal on the first head pin and go through the center link on a 17-in. chain. String 1 SC and go through the center link of the other 17-in. chain. String 1 MC and go through the center of the 11-in. chain. String 1 AC and go through the center of the 9-in. chain. String 1 MC and the dangle and make a small loop below it, wrapping around the roundnose pliers' jaw 2-3 times (**photo a**).

❸ Make a row of beads on each side of the center as follows: String 1 MC, skip 2 links, and go through the third. String 1 SC, skip 2 links, and go through the third. String 1 MC, skip 2 links and go through the third. String 1 AC, skip 3 links, and go through the fourth. String 1 MC and make a double loop below it (**photo b**).

❹ Make a dangle row on each side with the same spacing on the chains as in step 3 but end with a dangle bead as in step 2.

❺ Repeat steps 3 and 4 six more times for a total of 15 dangles. End after working step 3 once more.

❻ Trim the 9-in. chain so no links remain on each end (**photo c, top**).

❼ Work 8 rows on each side, repeating step 3 through the AC crystal and making a double loop below the AC crystal (**photo c**). Cut off the remainder of the 11-in. chain on each end.

❽ Work 10 rows on each side, using the first three crystals of the pattern in step 3. Or work enough rows to make the necklace the desired length minus the clasp (mine is 16 in./41cm).

❾ Attach a split ring to the fourth link from the last row on each chain. Do not

a

b

c

cut off the excess chain until you've finished the necklace and are sure it's the right length.

❿ Making sure the necklace is not twisted, attach each split ring to a loop on the clasp (**photo d**). Try on the necklace for length. If it needs lengthening or shortening, remove the split rings from the chain and make the necessary changes. Then re-attach the clasp to the chain. Finally, cut off the excess chain.

⓫ Optional: Using 2 pieces of scrap wire, make a double loop on the end of each to serve as a head. Hang an MC and an SC crystal on each wire. Attach one dangle to each of the bottom split rings with a wrapped loop (see "Basics," p. 136—**photo e**). ◗

d

e

materials

- 4½-5 ft. (1.4-1.5m) 2.2mm Cable chain
- **70-80** Thin or ultra-thin head pins or 11-13 ft. (3.4-4m) 24-gauge wire
- **1** 8-in. (20cm) Strand pressed-glass beads
- **167-187** 4mm Round Swarovski crystals, main color (MC)
- **67-77** 4mm Round Swarovski crystals, second color (SC)
- **47** 6mm Round Swarovski crystals, accent color (AC)
- **13-15** Dangles with vertical hole or hole across top (we used oblong stick pearls)
- **1** Two-strand filigree clasp
- **4** 4mm Split rings

Pin frills

Trim a brooch finding with a fringed border

by Pam O'Connor

The interesting 4-hole pin finding above seemed to deserve more than a ho-hum dangle or two suspended from each hole. It needed something more substantial, but what? Then—Eureka!—it hit me. This pin needed fringe—an *interesting* fringe.

After I completed the silver pin, fringe enthusiasm inspired me to make a second pin. I started with the same brick-stitch base and dressed it up with a frilly branched fringe.

stepbystep

Begin each pin with a brick-stitch ladder of bugle beads and 3-cut or hex-cut beads. For the silver pin, the ladder is attached to the 4-hole pin finding before adding the fringe. I glued the pin finding to the back of the lavender ladder after adding the fringe.

silver pin

❶ Thread a needle with 4 ft. (1.2m) of Nymo and string 2 bugle beads. Leave a 6-in. tail (15cm) and go through both beads again in the same direction. Pull the top bead down so the beads are side by side. The thread exits the bottom of bead #2. String bead #3 and go back through #2 from top to bottom (**figure 1**). Come back up through bead #3.

❷ String bead #4. Go through #3 from bottom to top and #4 from top to bottom. Add odd-numbered beads like #3 and even-numbered beads like #4 (**figure 2**). There are 23 bugles in this row to match the length of the pin finding.

❸ To stabilize the ladder, zigzag back through it (**figure 3**).

❹ Make a second row with 9º 3-cut beads: String 2 beads. Go under the thread between the 2nd and 3rd beads on the ladder from back to front. Pull tight. Go up the 2nd bead added then down the first. Come back up the second bead again (**figure 4**).

❺ For the remaining stitches on the row, pick up 1 bead at a time. Pass the needle under the next loop on the row below from back to front and go back through the new bead (**figure 5**).

❻ To attach the brick-stitch ladder to the pin, line up the row of 3-cut beads under the finding and determine which beads fall under the holes in the pin. Zigzag through the beads and out the top of the bead under the first hole. Go through the hole in the pin finding and sew through the next bead (**photo a**). Circle back through the bead you first exited and go through the hole and the next bead again. Repeat a third time.

❼ Zigzag through the 3-cut beads, exiting the bead under the second hole. Secure as in step 6. Repeat for the third and fourth holes.

❽ Zigzag through any remaining beads, exiting the bottom of the last 3-cut bead. Sew through the end bugle.

❾ Plan your fringe to coordinate with the finding. I wanted a long fringe with an arrowhead bead beneath each of the pin's three moon designs. For a symmetrical design, I counted from the center bugle bead (#12), determining which 2 bugles were beneath the first and third moons and equidistant from the center bugle (#5 and #18).

⑩ String the first fringe. The short fringes are made with 5 black 3-cut beads, a green 8º seed bead, and another 3-cut. Skip the last 3-cut and sew back through the fringe beads and the bugle. Sew down through the next bugle and add another fringe.

⑪ Below the 5th, 12th, and 18th bugle beads, string a fringe with 5 3-cuts, an 8º seed bead, 3 3-cuts, an arrowhead bead, and a 3-cut. Skip the last 3-cut and sew up the fringe and the bugle (**photo b**). Add fringes until the row is finished.

⑫ Zigzag through a few bugles and sew down a few beads on a fringe. Tie a half-hitch knot (see "Basics," p. 136) and glue with G-S Hypo cement. Sew down two more beads. Tie another half hitch and glue. Sew out the bottom of the fringe and trim close to the beads.

⑬ Finish the beginning thread tail as in step 12.

lavender pin

❶ Sew a ladder with 20 bugles as in steps 1-3 above.

❷ Add a row of 8º hex-cut beads as in steps 4-5 above.

❸ After you complete the row of hex-cut beads, sew down the end bugle, pick up 8 beads, mixing the Japanese cylinder beads with a few accent beads from your bead medley. I selected pinks, greens, and blues to coordinate with the iridescent purple cylinder beads.

❹ Skip the last bead and sew up a few beads on the fringe. String 3 or 4 beads from the mix of cylinder and medley beads. Skip the last bead and sew back up the beads added and a few more beads up the main strand. Add 2 more branches in this manner and sew through the remaining beads and the bugle bead.

❺ Sew down the next bugle. Add another branched fringe. The first half of this pin's graduated fringe has 3 8-bead branched strands, 3 12-bead branch strands, and 4 15-bead branched strands. Reverse the order for the second half.

❻ To end a thread, complete a fringe and sew back to the previous fringe. Tie a

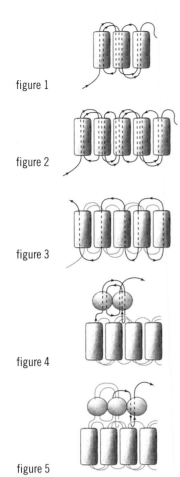

figure 1

figure 2

figure 3

figure 4

figure 5

half-hitch knot a few beads down the fringe and glue with G-S Hypo cement. Sew through a few more beads, tie another half hitch, and glue. Sew through a few beads and trim the thread close to the beads. Add thread by sewing up the last fringe added, tying and gluing half-hitch knots every two or three beads. Sew through the bugle and down the next bugle to begin adding more fringe.

❼ Complete the row of fringe and end the thread as in step 6.

❽ Cut a piece of interfacing slightly smaller than the bugle bead ladder. Cut a piece of Ultrasuede the same size as the interfacing. Glue the interfacing to the back of the bugle beads with Bond 527. Center and glue the pin finding onto the the interfacing.

❾ Cut slits in the Ultrasuede to accommodate each end of the pin backing. Apply a thin layer of glue to the pin and interfacing and position the Ultrasuede over the pin and interfacing (**photo c**). Allow the glue to dry completely before wearing your pin. ●

a

b

c

materials

both pins
- Nymo D, in coordinating color
- Beading needles, #10
- G-S Hypo cement

silver pin
- 1 4-Hole pin finding, sterling silver (available from Rishashay, 800-517-3311)
- 23 5mm Bugle beads, matte black
- 1 Tube (10g) 9º 3-cut beads, jet black
- 3 10 x 12mm Stone arrowhead beads, moss agate
- 24 8º Seed beads, green

lavender pin
- 20 7mm Bugle beads, iridescent lavender
- 20 8º Hex-cut beads, metallic purple
- 1 Tube (10g) Japanese cylinder beads, lilac
- 1 Tube (10g) seed bead medley
- 1 1-in. (2.5cm) Pin finding
- Pellon medium-weight nonfusible interfacing
- Ultrasuede in coordinating color
- Bond 527 cement

Unforgettable bracelets

Random or regular, memory wire cuff bracelets are fun and easy

by Louise Malcolm

String two or three feet (61-91cm) of beads in varying shapes and sizes onto memory wire and, in almost no time, you'll have a fabulous coiled cuff bracelet. The random cuff (above) will feel substantial and will be sure to draw attention. The pearl cuff (opposite below) has a dressier look. Memory or Remembrance wire is steel spring wire that always returns to its original coil shape and size. It comes in necklace, bracelet, and ring sizes, but the bracelet size is the most popular.

The key thing to remember about memory wire is that it will destroy jewelry-grade wire cutters. As an alternative, cut it with the heavy-duty wire cutters from the family tool chest. Or grasp it with chain- or flatnose pliers and bend the wire back and forth two or three times until it snaps.

stepbystep

random cuff

❶ Break off a length of memory wire 5-7 turns long. Make a loop in one end as follows: Grasp the end of the memory wire about a third of the way from the tips of your roundnose pliers. You should not be able to feel the end of the wire between the pliers' jaws. Rotate the pliers as far as your wrist will turn. Regrasp the loop at the same place in

a

b

c

d

e

the jaws and continue turning until the loop is closed tightly. If possible, turn it a little past closed (**photo a**).

❷ Make a mix of your assorted beads and seed beads and string them randomly on the end without the loop. String so that the big beads are slightly offset, and fill in between the accent beads with seed beads.

❸ Wrap the coil of beads around your wrist periodically to make sure the accent beads are offset and the spaces between them fill in nicely. When the bracelet is as long as you want it, break off the excess wire, leaving about ½ in. (1.3cm). Turn another loop at this end.

❹ String dangles with some of the leftover beads on the four head pins. Make a loop or wrapped loop above the beads (see "Basics," p. 136).

❺ Attach a charm to each of the eyes on the eye pins or to eyes made at the ends of the cut-off pieces of head pin. String a few beads and make an eye above them. Hang half the dangles on the loop at one end of the bracelet and the other half on the loop at the other end (**photo b**). Open and close the eyes on the dangles as shown in "Basics."

pearl cuff

❶ Grasp the memory wire with chainnose pliers where you want it cut. This will be about 1⅓ turns or 6½-7 in. (16.5-18cm). Break off four equal pieces and glue a 3mm memory wire stop bead on one end of each wire. Let the glue dry for 5-10 minutes.

❷ For the first wire, string 1 rondelle, 4 pearls, and 1 rondelle. Go through an end hole on one of the spacer bars.

❸ String 1 rondelle, 3 pearls, and 1 rondelle and go through an end hole on the second spacer bar. Repeat this stringing pattern. Then go through an end hole on the third spacer bar. String

materials

random cuff
- 36 in. (9cm) Bracelet memory wire
- Assorted beads with holes that will fit on the memory wire (a great use for leftovers)
- 7g Size 6º seed beads
- **4** Head pins
- **4** Eye pins (or leftover wire from head pins)
- **4** Small charms

pearl cuff
- **1** 16-in. (41cm) Strand 8mm simulated South Sea pearls
- **3** 4-Hole silver spacer bars (both from Rio Grande, 800-545-6566)
- **1** 16-in. Strand faceted rondelles, 5 x 7mm
- **8** 3mm Half-drilled memory wire stop beads (Beadalon)
- **4** Coils 1⅓-turn-long bracelet memory wire
- Gap-filling cyanoacrylate glue (Zap-A-Gap or Insta-Cure +)
- **Tools:** round- and chainnose pliers

the pattern in step 2 in reverse.

❹ Snug up the beads then break off the excess memory wire, leaving ⅛ in. (3mm) (**photo c**).

❺ Place a drop of glue on the end of the wire and immediately put a stop bead over the glue (**photo d**). Hold the piece for 1-2 minutes until the glue is set.

❻ String the second wire as follows: 2 rondelles, 3 pearls, 2 rondelles and go through the second hole on the first spacer bar. String 2 rondelles, 2 pearls, and 2 rondelles and go through the second hole on the middle bar. Repeat this pattern, go through the second hole on the last bar, and reverse the first pattern. Repeat steps 4-5 to end the wire.

❼ Repeat steps 2-6 for the third (**photo e**) and fourth wires. **❍**

Knot hard

Use tweezers to perfect your bead knotting skills

by Sarah K. Young

For hundreds of years, people have been stringing pearls and semi-precious stone beads on silk with knots between each bead. The knots protect the beads by keeping them from rubbing against each other. If a necklace breaks, one bead might slip away, but the knots will hold the rest together. Knots also enhance the design by spacing beads slightly so their shape and color show to best advantage. Silk is ideal because it drapes better than any other kind of cord; for stones and other beads that may have sharp holes, nylon beading cord is a good alternative.

stepbystep

Before you launch into your first knotting project, make a sample piece to practice the technique. Knotting isn't difficult; untying knots is. So be sure you can land that knot in the right place every time.

❶ Determine the finished length of the necklace. Cut the beading cord 5 times the finished length and use it doubled.

❷ String the beads and move them to about 10 in. (25cm) from the tail end. Knot the tails temporarily around the end bead to keep the beads on the cord. If you are working with graduated beads or have a centered design, set aside about 1½ in. (3.8cm) of beads at each end so you can adjust the length before finishing the necklace.

❸ Working about 10 in. from the needle end of the cord, make an over-hand knot (see "Basics," p. 136). Slide a bead tightly against the knot. You should have at least 12 in. (30cm) of cord between this bead and the others.

❹ Hold the bead in your left hand and loop the cord around the middle three fingers of your left hand. Drop the bead through the loop from back to front. To keep the knots slanted in the same direction, make every knot exactly the same (**photo a**).

❺ With the knotting tweezers in your right hand, reach through the loop and grab the cord right next to the bead with the tweezers' tip (**photo b**). Keep the tweezers perpendicular to the cord or you'll damage it on the tweezers' edges.

❻ Once you have a secure grip on the cord, let the loop slide off your fingers.

With your left hand, pull the cord slowly so the knot slides toward the bead. Use your thumbnail to push the knot into place next to the bead (**photo c**). Remove the tweezers and pull on the cord to tighten the knot. Grab the individual cords and pull them apart gently to tighten the knot and push it against the bead (**photo d**).

7 Slide the next bead against the knot and repeat steps 4-6. Don't change your looping technique as the knotted strand grows, even though you'll be dropping more than a foot of beads through the loop. Continue until you have knots between all but the last few beads. Check the necklace's length and make any adjustments by removing beads or adding back the reserved beads from step 2 before you finish knotting. Be sure to make an overhand knot after each end bead.

8 String a bead tip onto the needle and cut the needle off the cord. Tie the tails with several surgeon's knots (see "Basics"), dab with nail polish, and trim the ends. Attach the hook on the bead tip to the clasp loop. Repeat on the other end of the necklace.

knotting tips

1 Silk sizes are usually designated by a letter—from O or A (thinnest) to FFF (thickest), with F (medium) the most commonly used size. Nylon beading cord is designated in numbers—from 0 (thinnest) to 6 (thickest).

2 The size of the holes in pearls and semi-precious stones varies greatly, but it's crucial to know what you're working with before you purchase your cord. If the silk or beading cord is too thin, the knots will slip uselessly into the beads. If it's too thick, you can't string beads. Always string on doubled cord.

3 Start with a longer piece of silk or cord than you think you'll need. Knots take up a surprising amount of material, so work with 5 times the length of the finished necklace. If you run short, the only solution is to start over.

4 Choose a cord color slightly deeper in tone than the predominant bead color, unless the thread color is part of the design. White or light-colored pearls are usually strung on white or ivory silk.

5 If stones have been drilled from

opposite sides, the hole will be much narrower in the center. Use a thin thread, but tie double knots so they won't slip into the bead hole. To make a double knot, pass the bead twice through the overhand loop before gripping the cord with tweezers (**photo e**).

6 For stones that have larger holes on one side, string them all small-side first. The knot will be swallowed if two large holes are adjacent.

7 If your design incorporates metal beads, don't knot next to them because the metal will quickly fray the cords. To protect the cord, put a seed bead between the metal bead and the knot.

8 To extend the life of a silk knotted necklace: don't let it get wet; don't store it hanging; and don't apply perfume or hairspray while wearing it.

9 Periodically inspect the knots with a magnifying glass. If you see a bit of silk sticking out between beads, one of the strands has probably broken. Wear usually shows first near bead tips or metal beads. Restring the necklace.

10 Silk is strong and comes in many beautiful colors, but don't use it to string glass or ceramic beads. Their sharp edges will fray this natural fiber rapidly. String these beads on nylon beading cord.

about tweezers

Tweezers designed to remove splinters have rough gripping surfaces and will shred your silk. Buy proper ones from bead stores, jewelry supply catalogs, or medical supply houses. Use a fine sharpening stone to smooth the tweezers' edges, and you'll never break through the silk again. ◉

materials

- 1 16-18 in. (41-45cm) Strand semi-precious stones or pearls
- Silk thread or nylon beading cord, size to fit bead hole
- 2 Bead tips
- Clasp (this one comes from Eclectica, 262-641-0910)
- Clear nail polish
- Twisted wire beading needles
- Tools: Knotting tweezers with long, tapered points and smooth jaws, round- or chainnose pliers, bead design board (optional)

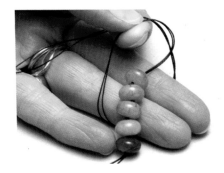

a

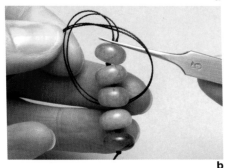

b

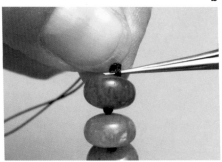

c

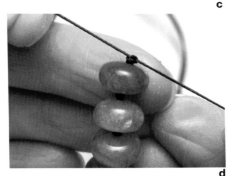

d

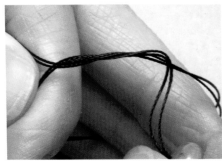

e

Use French wire

For a professional look

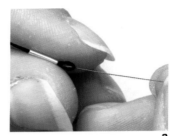

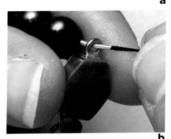

by Deb Gottlieb

French wire, also called bullion wire, is a fine gold or silver coil. It's a favorite of jewelers for finishing fine jewelry, so using it to finish a necklace immediately defines that necklace as precious. A small length of the coil covers the loop of cord that joins the strand to the clasp. The look is more elegant than a bead tip, and the wire protects the cord from wear.

Bullion wire comes in several diameters. Choose a size that will allow your cord to pass through when doubled. The wire is easily crushed or snagged, so store it in a plastic tube or box.

stepbystep

❶ Set aside the 8 pearls with the largest holes for the beginning and end of the necklace. You will have to thread through the end pearls twice. If necessary, enlarge the holes with a broach (a small needle file), a motor tool, or a flexible shaft machine.

❷ String 3 large-holed pearls on doubled silk and slide them to 3-4 in. (7.6-10cm) from the end of the cord. Do not knot the end.

❸ Cut a ¼-⅜-in. (6mm-1cm) length of French wire, using sharp scissors or wire snips. Support the wire between your fingertips as you thread it onto the silk and slide it all the way to the pearls (**photo a**). Squeeze slightly to prevent the wire's snagging on the needle eye.

❹ Thread through the eye on the clasp and position it in the middle of the French wire (**photo b**).

❺ Thread through the first pearl again pointing toward the tail. Pull slowly and firmly to close the French wire loop (**photo c**). Do not let the thread twist because it can clog the wire and stretch the coil. Also keep the wire straight as long as possible to prevent it from kinking before the loop closes.

❻ Tie an overhand knot against the first pearl with all four cord strands (**photo d**).

❼ Thread through the second pearl and tie another overhand knot.

❽ Go through the third pearl and tie a front-back-front knot ("Basics," p. 136).

❾ String the fourth large-holed pearl, all the regular pearls, and the other 4 large-holed pearls. Knot after every pearl, stopping after the fifth pearl from the end.

❿ Repeat steps 3-5 to attach the other end of the strand to the clasp with French wire.

⓫ Thread back through the last pearl, cut the needle off the cord and tie a front-back-front knot. Thread each tail on its own twisted wire needle and bring each back through the next pearl. Tie another front-back-front knot. Go through the third pearl and knot again. Finally, bring both tails through the fourth pearl and cut the thread off against the pearl.

⓬ Thread the starting tails onto two twisted wire needles and bring them through the fourth pearl before clipping them. If desired, dot the last front-back-front knot on each end with G-S Hypo cement or clear nail polish. ◦

materials

- Pearls or beads
- The thickest cord that passes 5 times through the largest-holed beads
- Bullion wire that accommodates doubled cord
- Twisted wire beading needles
- G-S Hypo cement or clear nail polish
- Tools: small broach (needle file); knotting tool of choice

Cone classics

Create elegant drop earrings with cones

by Pam O'Connor

Cones hold ice cream; they keep us out of construction lanes on the highway; they grow on pine trees—and they make killer drop earrings. Their sleek shape sets off large beads or crystals, creating earrings with a singular glamour.

Each of the bead choices here—a 10mm bead and a top-drilled, faceted crystal drop—requires a different tactic to achieve the look.

stepbystep

Coordinate your selection of cones and beads to be sure the focal bead or crystal fits into the cone.

red bead earrings

❶ Place a round bead on a decorative head pin. Slide the head pin into the cone, exiting the narrow end.
❷ String a silver bead onto the head pin (**photo a**).
❸ Make a loop or a wrapped loop (see "Basics," p. 136). Link this loop to the loop on the earring finding (**photo b**).
❹ Repeat steps 1-3 to make the second earring.

green crystal earrings

❶ Snip the head off a head pin or cut the 6 in. (15cm) of wire in half, reserving one half for the second earring.
❷ Make a perpendicular bend ½ in. (1.3cm) from one end of the wire. String the crystal on the long end of the wire.
❸ Bend up the long end of wire so it abuts the wire's opposite end at the crystal's tip (**photo c**).
❹ Straighten the remaining length of wire with chainnose pliers so it is in line with the central axis of the crystal (**photo d**).
❺ String the cone onto the wire, wide end first.
❻ Repeat step 3 for the red-bead earring.
❼ Repeat steps 1-6 for the second earring. ❍

materials

red bead earrings
- **2** 10mm Silver foil-lined glass beads
- **2** 22mm Bali silver cones
- **2** Sterling silver head pins with decorative ends
- **2** 4mm Silver beads
- **2** French wire sterling silver earring findings

green crystal earrings
- **2** 12mm Bali silver cones
- **2** Sterling silver head pins or 6 in. (15cm) of 20-gauge wire
- **2** French wire sterling silver earring findings
- **2** 20mm Faceted crystal drops, top-drilled
- Tools: Round- and chainnose pliers, diagonal wire cutters

a

b

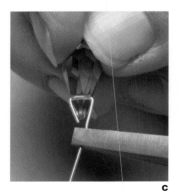

c

d

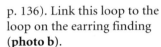

Beaded
links

Use eye pins to connect your favorite beads

by Jane Baird

An enduring style for beaded jewelry is a chain of beads linked with wire loops. It's great for necklaces of any length and for bracelets, too. The technique is versatile and requires only one skill—making loops (or eyes) with roundnose pliers (see "Basics," p. 136).

design tips

When designing your necklace or bracelet, remember to vary the color, size, shape, and texture of the beads to give the piece visual interest. Maintain enough consistency, however, to create a harmonious design. In this necklace, I

chose aqua as the dominant color, accenting it with amber, carnelian, and tortoiseshell glass beads.

I selected different sizes of beads and grouped the smaller ones together. Then I linked their eye pins in a random pattern. The recurring metal loops help provide an overall design consistency.

The bracelet above has a different design imperative, since the garnets set in sterling silver have a "right" side that needs to be face up. Because loops connect at a right angle, linking the bracelet's components to each other would cause the garnet pieces to skew. To prevent this, connect the loops with jump rings so the components remain in the same plane. Also, links on a bracelet should be 1 in. (2.5cm) or less so that the bracelet curves gracefully around your wrist.

stepbystep

It's quicker and easier to make the units first and link them afterwards. If you use purchased eye pins, save the trimmings for smaller elements. When using wire, cut off a workable length (about 1 ft./ 30cm) and make a loop on one end. String the bead(s) for the first unit and trim the wire to the proper length. Be sure to "flush cut" your wire on both ends for a professional look. A flush cut is achieved by holding the wire cutters with the flat side of the jaws toward the existing eye (see **photo c, p. 43**). Protect your eyes from airborne wire snips by wearing safety glasses. Loops on both sides of each eye pin should be on the same plane.

necklace and earrings

❶ Make the following eye pin units: 12 aqua diamonds with a seed bead on each end; 4 amber units—8mm aqua bead,

seed bead, amber bead, seed bead, 8mm aqua bead; 8 carnelian units—carnelian, tortoiseshell disc bead, carnelian; and 16 round aqua beads.

❷ Link the units in a random pattern. Use chainnose pliers to bend the end of one eye slightly to the side to link it to the next unit (**photo at bottom**). Rotate the end back into the plane with chainnose pliers to close the loop. Never bend the eye-pin loop out from its circular shape to link loops.

❸ For earrings, put a carnelian, a seed bead, a disc bead, and another seed bead on a head pin and make a loop. Make an aqua diamond eye pin unit as above. Link the head pin to the eye pin and the eye pin to the earring finding.

bracelet

❶ Make 5 eye pin units with a 3mm garnet bead, a silver rondelle, and another 3mm garnet bead.

❷ Link the eye pin units to jump or split rings (split rings are more secure). Link each jump or split ring unit to a silver-set garnet.

❸ Link the 5 linked eye pin and set garnet pieces to each other so that the eye pin and garnet units alternate. Thread the set garnets on the jump rings in the same direction so that they all face up.

❹ Attach a lobster claw clasp to one end of the bracelet and a ring to the other. ◉

materials

necklace
- **12** 20x14mm Diamond-shaped beads, aqua
- **4** 12mm Pentagonal cylinder-shaped beads, light amber
- **16** 8mm Faceted carnelian beads
- **8** 8mm Square disc beads, tortoiseshell
- **24** 8mm Round beads, aqua
- **32** 8° Seed Beads, silver-lined amber
- **33** Gold eye pins or 5½ ft. (1.7m) of 22-gauge gold-filled half-hard wire

earrings
- **2** 20x14mm diamond-shaped beads, aqua
- **8** 8° Seed beads, silver-lined amber
- **2** 8mm Square disc beads, tortoiseshell
- **2** 8mm Faceted carnelian beads
- **2** Eye pins
- **2** Head pins
- **1** Pair French hook earrings

bracelet
- **5** Sterling silver-set garnets or other stones
- **5** 8mm Sterling silver rondelles
- **10** 3mm Garnet or stone beads
- **9** Small silver jump rings or split rings
- **3** Extra-thin silver eye pins or 6 in. (15cm) of 24-gauge silver half-hard wire
- **1** Lobster claw clasp and ring

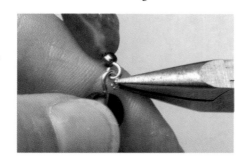

Easy as 1-2-3

It's easy enough to design different necklaces for different effects, but how do you create one versatile necklace that can be worn in variety of ways? This necklace is the answer. It can be classically simple or elaborate and glamorous. You can wear each strand separately or in combination with one or both of its companion strands. The key to joining the strands is using S-hook clasps. You'll need seven in all—a large, sturdy one for the main clasp and six smaller ones for the ends of each of the three strands.

Explore your options with this convertible, three-strand necklace

by Karen Smaalders

The three strands work well as a graduated or twisted necklace. Each strand is ⅝ in. (1.6cm) longer than the one above. Twisting, however, will shorten the necklace, so allow about 1 in. (2.5cm) of extra length (or more for larger beads). Because they are hooked into the same clasp at the back, you won't have a problem with clasps shifting, as you would wearing three separate necklaces. There are no limits to the variations on this theme. A gemstone and precious metal bead combination would be stunning. Or rummage through your leftover beads from other projects to find a starting point for the design. This necklace is an excellent way to put those wallflower beads back in circulation.

stepbystep

Decide the length of your shortest strand. Then make the second one ½ to ¾ in. (1.3-2cm) longer and the longest one 1 to 1½ in. (2.5-3.8cm) longer. Keep the lengths similar if you plan to wear them twisted and not graduated.

❶ Start each strand with a 50-in. (1.3m) length of bead cord. Thread a twisted wire needle and center it on the cord. String a silver spacer bead or 6º seed bead, leaving a 6-in. (15cm) tail. Go through a 4-5mm split ring and sew back through the bead.

❷ Tie a front-back-front knot (see "Basics," p. 80) with the tail strands. String another silver spacer bead or 6º seed bead. Use a second needle to sew both tail ends through this bead. Remove the second needle and tie another front-back-front knot. Dot the knots with glue.

❸ Sew both the working cord and the tail ends through a third spacer bead or 6º bead. Leaving the tail alone, string the necklace beads.

❹ I selected one type and size of pearl for each strand. To unify the design, I included pink silver-lined 6º seed beads, silver spacers, and opalescent 4mm glass beads in all three strands. The beads are strung in random order with a preponderance of pearls.

4a. String the short strand, using the smallest pearls, and finish as in step 5.

4b. String the middle strand with the medium pearls and finish as in step 5.

4c. String the long strand with the large pearls and finish as in step 5.

❺ To end each strand, string 3 silver spacers or 6º seed beads and go through a 4-5mm split ring. Sew back through the last spacer. Adjust the beads along the cord so that there are no thread gaps, but the beads drape well without stiffness. Cut off the needle, tie a front-back-front knot and glue it. Thread the needle on both cord ends and go through the next-to-last silver spacer. Tie another front-back-front knot and glue it. Thread the needle again and go through another bead or two. Clip the starting and ending tails. Hook an S-hook to each split ring.

wearing the necklace

To wear a single strand, link the two small S-hooks or attach them to the 5-6mm split rings on the large S-hook, as you would for a two- or three-strand necklace. Make sure the openings in all the S-hooks are as small as possible. To twist the strands, wrap the longest one around the two shorter ones until they're all about the same length. Then attach the small S-hooks to the split rings of the large S-hook clasp (see the detail photo above). ❍

materials

all necklaces
- Nylon beading cord, #1
- Twisted wire beading needles
- 1 Large sterling silver S-hook, 1¼ -1½ in. (3-4cm)
- 6 ¾-in. (2cm) Sterling silver S-hooks
- 6 4-5mm silver split rings
- 2 5-6mm silver split rings
- 18 Bali silver spacer beads
- G-S Hypo cement

short strand, 15¼ in. (39cm) plus clasp
- 1 16-in. (41cm) Strand 5mm freshwater pearls
- 25-30 4mm Faceted-quartz beads
- 25-30 4mm glass beads, opalescent white
- 25-30 6º seed beads, pink silver-lined

medium strand, 15⅞ in. (40cm) plus clasp
- 1 16-in. Strand 6-8mm freshwater pearls
- 20-25 6mm Faceted rose quartz beads
- 20-25 7mm Pressed-glass beads
- 20-25 6º seed beads, pink silver-lined

long strand, 16½ in. (42cm) plus clasp
- 25-30 8-10mm Freshwater pearls
- 12-15 10mm Faceted-glass beads
- 12-15 4mm Faceted-quartz beads
- 12-15 4mm glass beads, opalescent white
- 12-15 6º seed beads, pink silver-lined

Diamond ball earrings on a budget

Create glittering crystal spheres

Alice Korach

Ten-thousand-dollar earrings are not, and never will be, items that I can work into my budget. But who could resist a stunning ball of diamonds with a semi-precious stone drop? After hours of trying to recreate the effect with crystal beads, I suddenly realized that in 1995, for the tenth issue of *Bead&Button*, I had figured out how to make rice-pearl spheres. The technique should easily transfer to crystal beads, I thought. Not so.

My first two attempts used 4mm bicone crystals, but because their length and diameter are the same, I couldn't get them tight enough and tapered correctly. Finally I tried 3mm Czech fire-polished beads because they're longer than they are wide. The second version is what you see in a larger 4mm size above. The more petite version in 3mm beads is on p. 71. I've dangled crystals and pearls from my earrings, but they'd also be beautiful on their own.

a

d

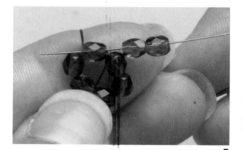

b

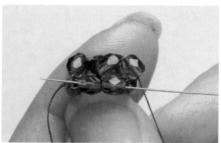

e

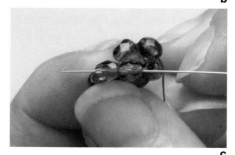

c

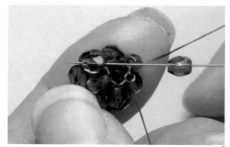

f

stepbystep

After weaving two "diamond" balls with faceted beads, attach them to each earring with a head pin (if you're not adding dangles) or an eye pin with small loops at each end. Suspend the dangle beads with eye and head pins. Use invisible thread (from a fabric store) if your crystals are transparent.

"diamond" balls

❶ Start with a 2-ft. (61cm) length of bead thread on a needle. String 6 faceted beads and, leaving a 6-in. (15cm) tail to weave in later, tie the beads into a tight ring using a surgeon's knot (see "Basics," p. 136).

❷ Go through the first bead and string 2 beads.

❸ Go through the first bead again in the same direction (**photo a**). Then bring the needle through the second bead on the circle.

❹ String 1 bead and go through the closer of the two beads strung in step 2 (**photo b**). Then go through the second and third beads on the circle (**photo c**).

❺ Repeat step 4 three more times. You will have 6 beads forming triangles on one side of the circle. After adding the sixth bead, continue through the same base bead and the first base bead on the circle (**photo d**).

❻ To connect the sixth bead to the first bead, go up the first bead and down the sixth (**photo e**).

❼ Continue either right or left through a circle bead and repeat steps 2-6 on the circle's other side.

❽ Follow a thread path through the center circle and out the top of any one of the upright beads on the first side. String 1 bead and go through the bead directly opposite the one you exited (**photo f**).

❾ Stitch back to an upright bead at the top of the second side and fill the hole with a bead as in step 8.

❿ Weave in both thread tails, tying several half-hitch knots between beads (see "Basics") and going through a bead before cutting the tails.

petite earrings

❶ Complete two diamond balls with 3mm faceted, fire-polished beads.

❷ Put a pearl drop bead on a head pin and make a small wrapped loop above it (see "Basics").

❸ Use the piece of wire that was left over from making the pearl drop to start a small wrapped loop and link it to the loop on the pearl before completing the wrap (**photo g**). Thread a 4mm crystal on the wire and make a small wrapped loop above it.

❹ Make a small wrapped loop on the end of a second head pin and cut off the head. Thread the wire through a diamond ball, going between beads on the center circle (**photo h**).

❺ Start a small wrapped loop below the ball and hook the loop above the crystal onto it before completing the wrap. Open the loop on the earring finding sideways and attach the loop at the top of the ball. Close the loop on the finding and make the second earring.

medium earrings

❶ Complete 2 diamond balls with 4mm fire-polished beads.

❷ String a 6mm crystal on a head pin and make a small wrapped loop above it. Make a small wrapped loop at one end of the remainder of the head pin. Thread the wire through the ball and begin another small wrapped loop below it. Before wrapping the lower loop, hang the crystal on it. Hang the top loop on the earring finding. Make the second earring to match. ●

materials

both earrings
- Beading needles, #12 or 13
- Nymo B, Silamide, or invisible thread
- Pair of earring findings with a loop
- Tools: round- and chainnose pliers, diagonal wire cutters

petite earrings
- **40** 3mm Fire-polished faceted Czech beads
- **4** Ultra-fine head pins (Beadworld, 206-523-0530)
- **2** 6-8mm Pearls for drops
- **2** 4mm Swarovski bicone crystals

medium earrings
- **40** 4mm Fire-polished faceted beads
- **2** Fine head pins
- **2** 6mm Swarovski bicone crystals

g

h

Summer spirals

Wrapped loops become bead caps for an airy choker   **by Alice Korach**

Several strands of large beads can make an uncomfortably heavy necklace. If you keep the strands of large beads short enough that they can be worn high on the neck, however, you'll produce a comfortable necklace that will make a bold statement as it draws attention to your face. To add interest to this four-strand, large-bead necklace, I chose two distinctly different shapes of beads. I kept the colors related with a primary (yellow) and one of the secondaries that can be made from it (green). Notice also that the yellow is a very soft shade while the green is a much more saturated, bold shade. You would get a similar effect by combining blue and lavender, pink and purple, or red and coral. When picking bead shapes and colors for a project like this one, the key is to think in terms of "related but different."

By stringing the beads together with wrapped loops, I provided spaces between them, as well as a metallic accent. Spacing out the beads in this fashion gives them more importance than they would have when run together because your eye takes in every single bead. Separating them also decreases the weight of the necklace. Extending the wraps over the tops of the beads to form

caps provides a finishing touch—one that further appears to increase the importance of each bead.

stepbystep

❶ Attach a 4mm soldered jump ring to each 6mm split ring. Then attach each split ring to a loop on the clasp.

❷ To begin the first strand, cut a 6-in. (15cm) length of wire and make a right-angle bend in it 2½ in. (6.3cm) from one end. Begin a wrapped loop with the 2½ in. end of the wire at the bend, working through step 3 (see "Basics," p. 136). Attach this loop to one of the split rings on the clasp.

❸ Slide a green bead on the longer portion of the wire and work the first 3 steps of a wrapped loop above the bead (**photo a**). Both loops should be in the same plane.

❹ To hold the bead evenly between the loops, wrap both wire tails the same amount around the wire shafts on each side of the bead.

❺ Wrap the remainder of the first wire tail in a tight spiral to cup one end of the bead (**photo b**). Clip the remainder as close to the spiral as possible. File the rough burr off the cut end of the wire so it doesn't feel sharp and can't snag your clothing. Cup the other end of the bead with the other wire tail.

❻ Repeat steps 2-5 with a yellow bead, attaching it to the second loop on the green bead. Continue alternating beads until you have attached 9 yellow beads and 10 green beads. Attach the tenth green bead to the matching split ring on the other side of the clasp (**photo c**). (Note: you may need 10 beads of each color on each strand. Offset the colors.)

❼ The second strand has 10 yellow beads and 9 green beads and begins and ends with a yellow bead. Attach the first loop to the soldered jump ring on the

a

b

c

d

split ring to which the first strand is attached (**photo d**). End by attaching the last loop to the matching soldered jump ring. The jump rings lengthen the strand slightly to allow for the fact that the tenth yellow bead is a bit shorter than the tenth green bead on the first strand. (If you have 10 beads of each color, omit these rings.)

❽ Repeat steps 2-7 with the other pair of split and jump rings. ●

materials

- **38-40** 10mm Jade beads, yellow
- **38-40** 14 x 8mm Czech pressed-glass beads, olive green
- **13 yd.** (11.9m) 22-gauge Sterling silver wire, half-hard
- **4** 4mm Soldered sterling silver jump rings or split rings
- **4** 6mm Sterling silver split rings
- **1** 2-hole Clasp (ours is from Pacific Silver-works, 805-641-1394)
- Tools: diagonal wire cutters, round- and chainnose pliers, #2 jeweler's file

Create a tribal look

Bundle multiple strands to make a necklace with ethnic flair

by Karen Smaalders

Ethnic jewelry designs evoke images of early mornings at dusty outdoor markets, stalls overflowing with fragrant spices, stacks of brightly colored textiles, and steaming pots of unfamiliar foods with exotic flavors. My favorite ethnic designs come from Africa, a culture I often look to for inspiration.

The multi-strand necklace shown here is based on the massed bead necklaces worn in Central Africa, where the number of bead strings is a reflection of wealth. My version is lighter and less bulky, a combination of tribal flavor with Western restraint.

step by step

My necklace is just over 20-in. (50cm) long, but you can modify the length as you like. If you use curved cones, they should fall toward the back of your collarbone for the best overall shape.

materials

- **2** Hanks 10º or smaller seed beads
- 3 ft. (.9m) Gold-filled chain
- **2** 1-in. (2.5cm) Brass cones (Ashes to Beauty Adornments 505-899-8864) or cones with 10mm openings
- Mix of beads and spacers to complement main-color beads
- Brass clasp (Ashes to Beauty Adornments)
- Nymo D or Silamide to match main bead color
- **2** 4mm Split rings
- **2** 3-in. (7.6cm) Medium-gauge gold-filled head pins or 6 in. (15cm) medium-gauge half-hard gold-filled wire
- 4 ft. (1.2m) Nylon beading cord, #2 or 3
- Twisted wire beading needles
- Beading needles #10 or 12 (extra-long, if available)
- G-S Hypo cement
- Tools: Round- and chainnose pliers, diagonal wire cutters, split-ring pliers (optional)

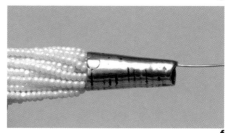

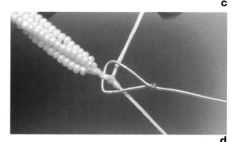

ends and tie the strands to the second triangle as in steps 4 and 6.

chain

❶ Attach a split ring to the middle of the chain and to one of the triangles holding the beaded strands (**photo e**). Hang the strands so they drape as if you were wearing them. (I attached mine to the handles on a vase.) Wrap the doubled chain around the strands three or four times and secure it temporarily to the triangle on the other side of the necklace.

❷ When you're satisfied with the way the chain wraps around the beads, trim off the excess links and attach the chain ends to another split ring. Attach this split ring to the second triangle.

finishing the back

Design the back of the necklace so the cones, beads, and clasp measure approximately 8½-in. (21cm).

❶ Insert the straight end of one of the headpins into the wide opening in one cone (**photo f**). Pull the wire through the cone until the beads sit tightly against the opening.

❷ With the wire extending from the cone's small hole, make a wrapped loop slightly larger than the opening to keep the wire from being pulled back through. If the small hole is more than ⅛-in. (3mm) wide, string a bead larger than the opening onto the head pin before you make the wrapped loop (**photo g, left**). Repeat on the other side of the necklace.

❸ Center one-half of the clasp on a 24-in. (60cm) length of bead cord and make an overhand knot close to the clasp's loop. Thread both cord ends through a twisted wire needle and string all but the last bead or two in this section. Set one of the cords aside. Using the other cord, string the last bead or beads, go through the wrapped loop made in step 2, and back through the last beads (**photo g**).

❹ Tie the two cords together with several surgeon's knots (see "Basics") (**photo h**). Glue the knots, take the tails through a neighboring bead, and hide the knots in the bead. Trim the tails.

❺ Repeat steps 1-4 to finish the other end of the necklace. ●

bead strands

❶ Determine the finished length of your necklace and the length you want to make the beaded strands. On the necklace shown on p. 74, the strands are 12-in. (30cm) long.

❷ Separate one strand of beads from the hank by cutting a thread near the knot. Working on doubled cord, transfer 12 in. of beads from the hank (**photo a**). Leave 6-in. (15cm) tails on each end. Tape the tails to your work surface or clamp them to keep the beads in place.

❸ Continue to transfer beads from the hank to your beading cord until you've strung enough strands to fill the cones. Keep checking as you work. My necklace required 24 beaded strands.

❹ Working with the strands on one side of the necklace, tie the cords together in groups of four, placing an overhand knot (see "Basics," p. 136) close to the end beads (**photo b**). Leave the other side untied for now.

❺ At the end of a head pin or 3 in. (7.6cm) of wire, make a wrapped loop (see "Basics") that will fit about halfway into a cone. With chainnose pliers, gently bend the loop into a triangle with a flat bottom and check that it still fits into the cone (**photo c**). Make a second triangle to match the first.

❻ Use several surgeon's knots (see "Basics") to tie each cluster of strands to the bottom of one triangle (**photo d**). Glue the knots and trim the threads to ¼ in. (6mm).

❼ Before you tie knots on the unfinished end of the necklace, add or remove beads from the strands to make them uniform in length. Then knot the

Chained dangles

An invisible connection

by Alice Korach

Earrings that feature dangles suspended on fine chain are all the rage these days. I wanted a pair of pearl chained earrings but I wasn't so crazy about the price. I knew I could get the parts from one of my favorite Bali silver importers, Rishashay (800-517-3311), but how was I to link the dangle and the earring to the chain securely and unobtrusively without soldering?

The trick is obvious once you know it (see steps 3-5). All it requires is a bit of patience and some manual dexterity. Medium-length fingernails also help.

stepbystep

If your pendants come with loops, you make two tiny 1¼ revolution jump rings to link the ends of a section of fine chain to a pendant and an earring loop. If you use beads and head pins for the pendants, you'll only have to make one tiny over-rotated jump ring per earring.

❶ Cut two 10-link lengths of chain or two pieces of the desired length.

❷ If you're using beads for pendants, string a bead on a head pin and make a wrapped loop through step 3 (see "Basics," p. 136). Stop before wrapping the loop. Catch the end link of a chain section in the loop and wrap once. Clip the wire tail off flush.

❸ With the excess wire, form a loop with a diameter of slightly more than 2mm near the tip of a pair of roundnose pliers. Continue to wind the wire an extra quarter turn past a full circle (**photo a**). Cut off the excess wire while still holding the loop on the pliers.

❹ Slide a thumbnail between the wires where the loop is double and use your other thumbnail to pry the loop open the width of the earring loop.

❺ Hook the end link of a chain section onto the loop, then hook the open loop onto the earring loop (**photo b**). Press the sides of the loop back together by squeezing gently with chainnose pliers (**photo c**).

❻ Repeat steps 3-5 to attach a pendant that comes with a soldered loop to the other end of the chain. Then make the other earring.

triple dangle earrings

❶ Cut two pieces of chain in each length: ½ in. (1.3cm), ¾ in. (2cm), and 1 in. (2.5cm).

❷ Attach the small crystal to the shortest chain, the medium crystal to the middle length, and the large crystal to the long piece, as in step 2 above.

❸ Attach the other end of the three chains to a split ring or a 2.5mm 1¼-turn ring (step 3 above) and attach the ring to the loop on the earring. Make the other earring to match, stringing the chains in the opposite order. ●

materials

single dangle earrings
- Pair of post earrings with loop
- **2** Pendant beads with a loop or 2 beads and 2 head pins
- 1½ in. (3.8cm) Cable chain, 1.9mm
- **1** Thin or Ultra-thin head pin

triple dangle earrings
- Pair of post earrings with loop
- 5 in. (12.7cm) Cable chain, 1.9mm
- **2** 6-8mm Swarovski crystals or pearls
- **2** 5-6mm Swarovski crystals
- **2** 4mm Swarovski crystals
- **6** Thin head pins
- **2** 4mm Split rings, optional
- Tools: small-tipped roundnose pliers, chainnose pliers, wire cutter

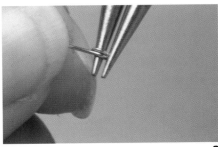

a

b

c

Elegant pearl lattice

Create crystal spacer bars for a classic bracelet

by Alice Korach

When I was a teen, my father returned from a trip to Japan with a gorgeous gift for my mother: a pearl and gold lattice bracelet. It has been put aside for the younger of my two nieces—lucky Rachel. When I recently saw an ad for a similar bracelet and necklace set, my design instincts went into high gear.

The trick to making a lattice-style piece of jewelry is to create a finding for the vertical spacer bars of the pattern. Here, I used 4mm fire-polished beads. Gold or silver beads would also work well. The only requirement is that the beads used on the spacer bars have large enough holes to accommodate two passes of an ultra-thin head pin or 28-gauge half-hard wire.

stepbystep

After making 10-13 crystal spacer bars, you link them together with pearls on wrapped loops. Then you link the pearls at the beginning and end of the bracelet strip to the clasp. It's critical that all the loops are the same size, so mark your roundnose pliers with a Sharpie.

making the spacer bars

❶ Cut the head off an ultra-fine head pin and make a small loop (about ⅛ in. / 3mm across) in the middle of the pin, working near the tips of your round-nose pliers. Use chainnose pliers to bend the wires below the loop so they extend straight down from the center of the loop (**photo a**).

❷ Thread a crystal on both wires, then spread the wires. Place one jaw of the roundnose pliers in the loop and the other lightly against the bottom of the crystal between the wires, holding the pliers straight so the loops will be the same size (**photo b**).

❸ Bend each wire around the side of the jaw and across the top so they point in opposite directions (**photo c**).

❹ Use chainnose pliers to bend each wire at a right angle so they are parallel and centered over the middle of the

a

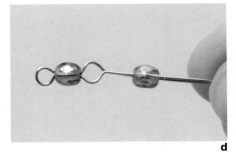

d

g

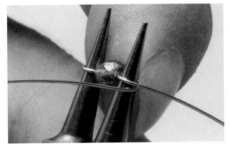

b

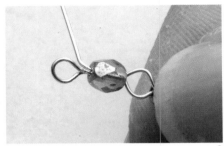

e

h

c

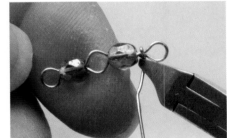

f

i

loop. Thread another crystal on both (**photo d**).

❺ Use one wire to form the loop part of a wrapped loop (see "Basics, p. 136) with a very short stem between the loop and the crystal. Finish the loop by bending the end so it sits parallel to the stem and cut off the excess so the wire end butts against the crystal (**photo e**).

❻ Use the other wire to wrap once around the stem and the tail of the loop wire. Then trim it as close as possible (**photo f**). Make 9-12 more spacer bars.

assembling the bracelet

❶ Start a wrapped loop with an ultra-fine head pin (if you are very careful, you can get two pieces from one head pin), leaving enough tail to wrap once (about ¼-in. / 6mm). Thread a pearl on the pin and start a wrapped loop on the other side of the pearl. Both loops must be in the same plane. Adjust them if necessary. Prepare two more pearls.

❷ Attach one pearl to each of the loops on the first spacer bar, completing these

three wrapped loops and trimming the wire tails as close as possible.

❸ Prepare 3 more pearls and attach them to the other side of the loops on the first spacer bar.

❹ Now comes the tricky part: You need to attach the next spacer bar to the other loops of the second set of pearls, making sure that none of the loops is twisted. Attach the middle pearl to the second spacer bar first.

Hold the bar up so the pearls dangle below it and the loops of the bar face you. Hold an end pearl against the matching end bar loop to see how the pearl needs to face (**photo g**).

For the pearl to end up properly oriented, you must thread it through the loop backward. If the wire tail needs to end up facing away from you, you must insert it through the loop, starting behind the loop with it facing toward you. If inserting diagonally left to right doesn't work, try inserting diagonally right to left (**photo h**). Occasionally, even though you have inserted the pearl

materials

- **50-75** Ultra-thin head pins (exclusive of Beadworld, 206-523-0530)
- **18mm** Sliding bar clasp, with loops
- **1** 16-in. (41cm) Strand 5-6mm nearly round freshwater pearls
- **30-39** 4mm Fire-polished Czech beads
- Tools: round- and chainnose pliers, diagonal wire cutters; Sharpie marker optional

correctly, it will look twisted. In this case, you need to bring the wire tail through the space between the end and middle pearls. Only when you're sure the pearl is oriented correctly is it safe to wrap the loop.

❺ Repeat with the other end pearl.

❻ Repeat steps 3-5, ending with step 3 when the bracelet is ¼ to ½ in. (.6 to 1.3cm) longer than your wrist circumference. The clasp will add another ½ in.

❼ Finish the wrapped loops on the end pearls, attaching them to the clasp loops (**photo i**). Before wrapping, make sure that the bracelet is not twisted. ●

Create a lariat with
pizzazz

*Reinvent your toggle
as a centerpiece*

by Kelly Charveaux

The simplest and most ancient of fastenings, a toggle, consists of a ring on one end and a bar on the other. A silver toggle focal point gives a necklace dramatic impact as well as a southwestern flair. Two of my favorite choices are using a stone donut and one of my original cast-silver bars or a large silver ring and a bar. You can accent the donut or silver ring with a few dangles, as in the turquoise necklace at left.

stepbystep

These directions can be used for both the stone donut or silver ring toggle necklace. Omit steps 1-2 to make a necklace without dangles.

❶ If using a stone donut, measure the distance from the outer edge of the donut to the hole and double it. On 10 in. (25cm) of flexible beading wire, string 11º seed beads or silver hexes to reach this measurement. String the wire through the donut hole or ring. Add or remove beads so that the bead loop reaches snugly from the edge, through the hole, and back to the edge. Bring the wire ends through two crimp beads, closing the loop (**photo a**). Crimp securely. String a large-hole bead, sliding it over the crimps (**photo b**).

❷ String about 1⅛ in. (2.8cm) of spacers, a large-hole bead, 1-2 crimp beads, 3 stone or accent beads, and a seed bead. The first few beads should cover both wires. Then trim the short end. Skip the seed bead and go back through the stones and the crimp beads. Hold the large-hole bead away from the stones, exposing the crimp bead(s). Crimp (**photo c**) and slide the large-hole bead over the crimps. Make a second dangle.

❸ On 23 in. (58cm) of flexible beading wire, string the same measurement of small beads as in step 1. String 1-2 crimp beads, leaving a 1½-in. tail at the starting end. String the wire through the donut hole or ring. Add or remove seed beads to fit and bring the tail through the crimps. Crimp then string a large-hole bead (**photos a** and **b**).

❹ String an accent bead and a few more beads over both wires. Then trim the tail. Now randomly string spacers and stones. When you reach 3-4 in. (7.6-10cm) from the end, string an accent bead, a few small beads, a large-hole bead, and 1-2 crimp beads.

❺ String the same measurement of small beads as in step 1 and the bar half of the toggle clasp. If the loop on the bar will not slide over these beads, string half the small beads, the bar and the other half of the small beads. Pass the wire end through the large-hole bead and the crimp beads (**photo d**). Push the large-hole bead toward the toggle bar, exposing the crimp beads. Crimp securely and trim the wire. ●

a

b

c

d

materials

- 1 Stone donut or silver ring
- 1 Silver bar long enough to secure the toggle (Scottsdale Bead Supply, 480-945-5988)
- 1 Strand of silver spacers
- 1 Strand of turquoise nuggets or stone beads
- 1 Hank of size 11º seed beads or a strand of 2.5mm Bali silver hex beads
- 1-4 Accent beads
- 6 Silver beads, 3mm or larger, with holes large enough to fit over a crimp bead
- 10-12 Crimp beads
- 1½ yd. (1.35m) Flexible beading wire, .019
- Tools: diagonal wire cutter, crimping tool

Fine feathered friends

Match your beads with a few feathers for a hip ensemble

Sad to say, it's hard to find an occasion to wear a feathered boa these days. If you want to add the flutter of feathers to your wardrobe, however, this necklace and earring set lets you do so with flair.

stepbystep

Decorative feathers can be found where fly-fishing supplies are sold. The ones used here are pheasant feathers.

make the earrings

1 Measure a feather from the tip and cut it to 1½ in. (3.8cm) in length. Starting from the cut end, trim ½ in. (1.3cm) of the barbs from the quill (**photo a**).

2 Apply a drop of E6000 glue to the trimmed end of the quill and insert it into the faceted rondelle (**photo b**).

3 With the wrong side of the feather facing you, insert the head pin into the rondelle (**photo c**). Allow the glue to dry before proceeding.

4 String a silver spacer and three 4mm beads onto the head pin and over the end of the feather. Make a small wrapped loop (see "Basics," p. 136) at the top of the head pin.

5 Repeat steps 1-4 twice to make 3 feather dangles.

6 Cut three 3-in. (7.6cm) lengths of 24-gauge wire. Make a small wrapped loop at one end of each wire.

7 Cut a 6-in. (15.2cm) length of flexible beading wire. String *a feather dangle, 2 silver beads, a wire with a wrapped loop, 2 silver beads* (**photo d**). Repeat * to * twice.

8 Remove the last silver bead strung and replace it with a crimp. Slide the other wire end through the crimp and tighten the wire into a cir-

cle (**photo e**). Leave enough ease so the dangles hang freely. Crimp the crimp (see "Basics") and trim the wire.

9 String a 4mm bead, a silver spacer, and a 4mm bead on one of the wires with wrapped loops. Start a small wrapped loop at the other end of the wire and slip a soldered jump ring into the wire before closing it (**photo f**).

10 String a 4mm bead, a spacer, and a 4mm bead onto the next wire on the circle. Trim the wire to ⅜ in. (1cm) above the beads and turn a loop at the wire's end (see "Basics"). Open the loop to the side and connect it to the soldered jump ring (**photo g**).

11 Repeat step 10 with the remaining wire.

12 Open the loop on an earring wire and insert the soldered jump ring into the loop before closing it (**photo h**).

13 Make a second earring to match the first.

make the necklace

1 Make seven feather dangles as described in steps 1-4 above with the following alterations: Use extra long headpins and the following bead counts—one 9-bead, two 7-bead, two 5-bead, and two 3-bead dangles.

2 Measure your neckline to determine the desired length. Subtract the clasp length and add 4 in. (10cm) for finishing. Cut a piece of flexible beading wire this length.

3 String the 9-bead dangle to the wire's center.

4 String a spacer and an 8mm bead on one wire end and an 8mm bead on the other end.

5 String a 7-bead dangle on each end of the wire.

6 String a spacer and an 8mm bead on the wire's ends.

7 Repeat step 5-6 with the

a

b

c

d

e

f

g

h

materials

earrings
- **6** Feathers
- **30** 4mm Stone beads
- **12** Bali silver spacers
- **16** 2mm Sterling silver beads
- **2** Crimp beads, sterling silver
- **6** Faceted stone rondelles
- **6** Head pins
- 18 in. (46cm) 24-gauge Sterling silver wire
- 12 in. Flexible beading wire, .014 or .013
- 1 Pair of earring findings
- E6000 glue

necklace
- **40** 4mm Stone beads
- **50-60** 8mm Stone beads
- **60-70** Bali silver spacers
- **7** Extra-long head pins
- Flexible beading wire, .019
- **1** Clasp

Tools: round- and chainnose pliers, diagonal wire cutters, crimping pliers

5-bead and 3-bead dangles.

8 String beads and spacers

alternately until you reach the desired length.

9 String a crimp and half the clasp on one end of the wire. Pass the wire back through the crimp and a few more beads. Crimp the crimp bead and trim the wire.

10 With the beads snug, repeat step 9 at the necklace's other end. ●—*P.O.*

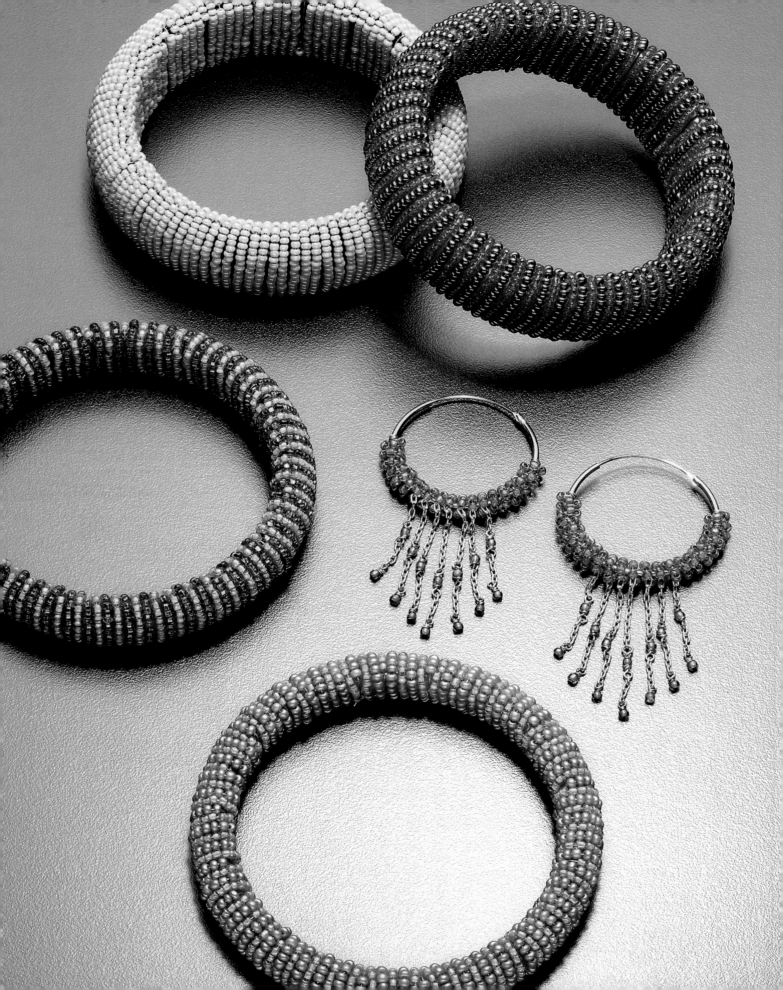

Beaded bangles

Wrap seed beads around inexpensive bangles and earrings

Thrift stores are a wonderful place to shop for inexpensive plastic bangle bracelets in various widths. When you're checking them over, don't worry about the color of the bangle or its finish. Buy one that's slightly large. When you wrap beads around it, the inside diameter will decrease. When you're done, only the beads will show. For the earrings, use thin hoops.

stepbystep

You wrap the beads around the bangle or hoops with craft wire. Since a little wire will show on the inside or at the seam of the two-color bangle, use neutral silver or gold or a matching color of Artistic or Color Craft wire.

one-color bangle bracelet

❶ String 4½-5 yd. (4-4.6m) of seed beads on the craft wire spool, leaving about 1 yd. (.9m) of unstrung wire at the beginning. Do not cut the wire from the spool. Wind the beaded wire around the spool to keep it from tangling and hold it in place with a rubber band.

❷ Wrap the end of the wire around the bangle and twist it tightly to itself along the edge of the bangle. Stretch the 1-2-in. (2.5-5cm) tail along the bangle in the opposite direction from the way you will be wrapping beads (**photo a**).

❸ Free about 18 in. (46cm) of beads and a yard of wire from the spool and wrap the beads completely around the bangle (**photo b**).

❹ Keep the wire tight as you wrap. As you need more wire and beads, unroll them from the spool, slide the beads down the wire, and roll up the excess, holding it with the rubber band. Every fifth or sixth wrap, do not put beads on the inside of the bangle (**photo c**). (Since the inside diameter of the bangle is smaller than the outside diameter, beads will mound up if you put them on every inside wrap.)

❺ When you near the starting tail, turn it toward the already wrapped part of the bracelet. Be careful not to flex it too much or it will break. When the last wrap of beads meets the first wrap, twist the starting and ending tails together (**photo d**). Then poke them under the bead wraps with an awl or tapestry needle (**see photo h**).

two-color bangle

❶ String 2½ yd. (2.3m) of beads of each color on its own spool of wire and wind up the spools as in step 1 above.

❷ Wrap both wires separately around the bangle as in step 2, above, but extend the tails in the direction you will be wrapping to cover them as you go.

❸ Wrap color A once around the bangle. When you get to the edge where the tails are twisted, twist the color A and the color B wire a tight half twist so that color B is now in advance of color A (**photo e**).

❹ Wrap once around with color B. Repeat the twist on the edge of the bangle to put color A ahead of color B, keeping both wires snug and fully beaded (**photo f**).

❺ Repeat steps 3 and 4, omitting beads on the inside of a wire every fourth to sixth wrap until the last color B wrap meets the first Color A wrap (**photo g**). Keep the twist lined up on the edge of the bangle.

❻ Twist the tails together and bury them under the bead wraps (**photo h**).

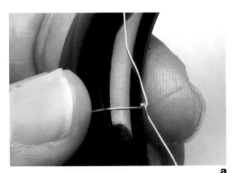
a

b

c

d

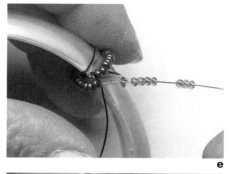

e

i

m

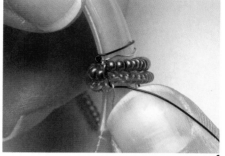

f

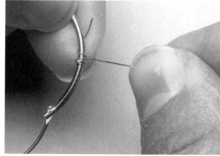

j

g

k

h

l

earring

Prepare the chain dangles first.

❶ Make two sets of dangles (**photo i**), working from bottom to top, as follows:

a. String 1 seed bead on each of 7 head pins and begin a tiny wrapped loop (see "Basics," p. 136). Leave about ½ in. (1.3cm) of wire for wrapping and cut off and reserve the rest of each head pin.

b. Pull the end of a 4-link chain into each loop and finish wrapping.

c. On a piece of reserved wire, begin a tiny wrapped loop and pull the other end of the 4-link chain into the loop before wrapping. String 1 seed bead on the wire and begin a tiny wrapped loop above it. Repeat with all seven dangles.

d. Add chain to the dangles as follows: Make 2 with 8-link tops, 2 with 6-link tops, and 2 with 4-link tops. Make the center dangle with a 10-link top.

❷ To bead the earring, cut a 1-yd. (.9m) length of craft wire and wrap the end 3-4 times tightly around the hoop a quarter of the way below the catch (**photo j**).

❸ String enough beads (40-50) to wrap over the tail and hoop to the bottom third, about 7 wraps. End with the wire at the bottom of the hoop and string one of the shortest dangles through the top chain link (**photo k**).

❹ Wrap the hoop once with beads, ending at the bottom, and string the next longer dangle. Repeat this step, graduating the dangles from shortest to longest and back to shortest (**photo l**).

❺ String enough beads to make the same number of wraps as you did at the beginning on the other side (**photo m**).

❻ End by wrapping bare wire 3-4 times tightly around the hoop against the last bead wrap. Then clip the wire off against the hoop. ❂—A.K.

materials

bracelet—one color
- ¾-in. (2cm) Plastic bangle bracelet
- **1** Spool 28-gauge craft wire
- 20g or **1** Hank 11º seed beads

bracelet – two color
- ¾-in. Plastic bangle bracelet
- **2** Spools craft wire
- **2** Colors of 11º seed beads, 10g each

earrings
- **1** Pair 1¼-in. (3cm) thin hoop earrings (about 1.5mm diam.)
- **1** Spool 28- or 30-gauge craft wire
- 3g 11º Seed beads
- **14** Thin head pins
- 15 in. (38cm) 2.2mm Cable chain

Tools: wire cutters, round- and chainnose pliers, rubber bands, awl or tapestry needle

Teardrop earrings

Oblong beads help emphasize the shape

My challenge in making these teardrop earrings was to figure out how to finish the ends of the beading wire. I knew I had to use crimp beads, but I also needed to have a loop turned in the right direction to hook onto the earring wires.

I solved that problem on the pair of malachite earrings by using silver end crimps, which are findings designed for leather and other thick cords. Luckily, the beads I chose had holes large enough to accommodate .024 beading wire. That gauge wouldn't go through the beads on the pearl earrings, however, so I switched to thinner beading wire and worked out an easy substitute for the end crimps—a soldered jump ring above a standard crimp bead.

stepbystep

Beading wire forms a teardrop shape when short lengths are brought together at the ends. Use oblong beads to reinforce the curves.

malachite earrings

❶ Cut two 7-in. (18cm) lengths of .024 flexible beading wire. You need a thick beading wire to fill the end crimps.
❷ Center a malachite bead on one piece of beading wire. String a 1¾-in. (4.4cm) pattern of bugle beads and spacers on each side of the central bead.
❸ Insert both ends of the wire into an end crimp (**photo a**) and slide the crimp close to the beads to form the teardrop shape.
❹ Turn the crimp so its loop is at a right angle to the beaded loop. (When you hang the finished teardrop on your earring wire, the beads should be parallel to the side of your head.) Use

crimping pliers to squeeze the end crimp around the beading wire (see "Basics," p. 136 and **photo b**). The cylinder of an end crimp is longer than an ordinary crimp, so you'll need to crimp twice to compress its full length.
❺ Trim the excess wire close to the end crimp with wire cutters.
❻ Open the loop on your earring wire as if it were a jump ring (see "Basics"), attach the teardrop, and close the loop.
❼ Make the second earring to match the first.

pearl earrings

❶ Cut two 7-in. lengths of .019 beading wire.
❷ Center a pearl on the wire. On each side of the central pearl, string 7 seed beads, a pearl, and 8 seed beads (or adapt these instructions to your own design).
❸ Insert both ends of the beading wire through a crimp bead and push the crimp against the beads. Take one wire end through a soldered jump ring and back through the crimp bead (**photo c**). (It's a snug fit.) Tighten the wires until you've removed all the slack.
❹ Keeping the jump ring at a right angle to the beaded loop (see step 4, above), crimp the crimp bead and trim the excess wire.
❺ Finish this earring as in step 6, above, and make the second earring to match the first. ●—*M.B.*

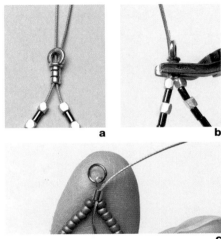

a

b

c

---

materials

malachite earrings
- 2 10x14mm Oval malachite beads
- 20 2mm Square Bali silver spacers
- 5g 3mm (size 1) Bugle beads
- Flexible beading wire, .024
- 2 End crimps
- 1 Pair earring wires with loop

pearl earrings
- 6 11 x 16mm Diamond-shaped freshwater pearls
- 5g Seed beads, size 11º
- Flexible beading wire, .019
- 2 Crimp beads
- 2 4mm Soldered jump rings
- 1 Pair earring wires with loop

Tools: wire cutters, crimping pliers

Strand multiplication

Add fullness to your stringing with necklace spreaders

These 3-to-1 necklace spreaders intrigue me. I love their ornate, ethnic flavor. For this necklace design, I wanted to make the spreaders visible, not hidden at the back of the neck near the clasp. A few large-hole silver beads and bead caps conceal the necklace's "mechanics." The spreaders proved to be the perfect accent for my shimmering green faceted pearls.

stepbystep

❶ Cut 3 pieces of .012 flexible beading wire with the following measurements: 20 in. (51cm), 19 in. (48cm), and 18 in. (46cm).

❷ String and center the beads on the wires in the following order:

   a. 5 in. (12.7cm) of pearls, 4 in. (10cm) of silver spacers, and 5 in. of pearls on the 20-in. wire.

   b. 4½ in. (11.3cm) of pearls, 3½ in. (8.9cm) of silver spacers, and 4½ in. of pearls on the 19-in. wire.

   c. 4 in. of pearls, 3 in. (7.6cm) of silver spacers, and 4 in. of pearls on the 18-in. wire.

❸ Thread the ends of the 20-in. wire through both spreaders' outside holes and out the single hole on the other side. Thread the 19-in. wire through the middle holes and the 18-in. wire through the inside holes. Tape the ends together at one end to keep them from slipping back through the spreader's holes (**photo a**).

❹ String 2 crimps over the untaped wire ends. Put the wire ends back through the crimps, making a ⅛ in. (3mm) loop (**photo b**). Crimp both crimp beads firmly (see "Basics," p. 136) and trim the excess wire.

❺ Take the tape off the wire ends on the other side and snug up the beads on all the wires. Repeat step 4 on this end of the necklace.

❻ Cut two 10-in. (25cm) pieces of .019 flexible beading wire. String a crimp to 3 in. from the end of one wire. Put the wire end through the 3-strand loop on one end of the necklace and back through the crimp. Tighten the loop and crimp (**photo c**).

❼ Repeat step 6 on the other end of the necklace.

❽ String a bead cap (cup up), a large-hole bead, a bead cap (cup down), a bead cap (cup up), a large hole bead and a bead cap (cup down) on one .019 wire, covering the crimps (**photo d**).

❾ String 5 in. of pearls and silver spacers in an alternating pattern on the wire. End with 2 or 3 spacers. String a crimp and half the clasp. Thread the wire back through the crimp and the spacers. Tighten the loop and crimp the bead. Trim the excess wire.

❿ Repeat steps 8-9 to complete the other side of the necklace. ●—*P. O.*

materials

- 20 in. (51cm) Flexible beading wire, .019
- 57 in. (1.4m) Flexible beading wire, .012
- 2 16-in. (48.2cm) Strands 5mm faceted pearls
- 1 16-in. Strand 4mm spacers, sterling silver
- 2 16mm 3-to-1 Sterling silver spreaders
- 4 Large-hole 8mm beads, sterling silver
- 8 Large-hole bead caps, sterling silver
- 1 Clasp
- 8 Crimp beads

Tools: crimping pliers, diagonal wire cutters

Centerpiece elegance

*Put your best beads up front and
hook them to wire sides*

If you're looking for an efficient way to show
off a few favorite or expensive beads, these
necklaces offer an unusual approach. Bend
heavy-gauge wire to hug the sides and back of
your neck. String your treasures across the
front. Use a series of large-hole beads to hide
the connection between the two sections.
Shape the wire ends into a hook-and-eye clasp.

stepbystep

neckwires—both necklaces

❶ Cut two 7-in. (18cm) lengths of 14-gauge wire.

❷ Using the tip of your roundnose pliers, turn a very small loop at one end of each piece of wire. If the loop is too large to fit inside into a large-hole silver bead, cut the wire tip on the diagonal (**photo a**) and flatten it slightly by pinching it with chainnose pliers (**photo b**) until it fits.

pearl necklace
knotting

❶ To string the pearls, cut a piece of cord 8 times the finished length of the front of the necklace (approximately 48 in. /1.2m for a 6 in./15cm finished length of pearls). Thread the twisted wire needle on the cord and use the cord doubled.

❷ String 5 in. (13cm) of pearls and move them to about 4 in. (10cm) from the tail end of the cord. Knot the tail temporarily to keep the beads from falling off. Make an overhand knot (see "Basics," p. 136) about 4 in. from the needle end and slide a pearl against the knot. Cut the needle off the cord.

❸ Hold the pearl in your nondominant hand and loop the cord around the middle three fingers of that hand (**photo c**). Drop the pearl through the loop and slip the cord off your fingers.

❹ Insert an awl (or other thin, smooth tool) into the loop, pointing it toward the needle end of the cord (**photo d**). Pull the cord slowly away from the awl to tighten the loop. Use the awl to slide the loop to the pearl (**photo e**). Push the loop off the awl with your thumbnail.

❺ Separate the cords and pull them apart to secure the knot against the pearl (**photo f**).

❻ Repeat with the remaining pearls.

❼ Tie one pair of cord ends to a loop on a neckwire using a surgeon's knot (see "Basics"). Glue the knot. Repeat with the other cord ends and neckwire.

❽ String two large-hole and one small-hole bead on the straight end of a neckwire. Push the first large-hole bead over the knot and loop to hide it (**photo g**). Slide the second and third beads against the first. Glue them together

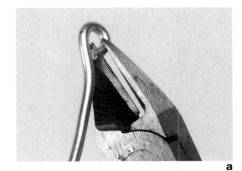
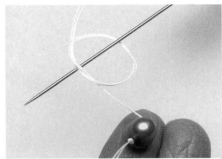

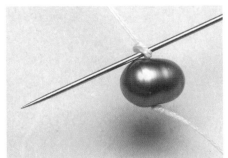

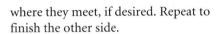

where they meet, if desired. Repeat to finish the other side.

clasp and shaping

❶ Shape the neckwires into semi-circles with your fingers. Hold the necklace around your neck to determine its finished length and mark the spot where the two wires cross. You may want to cut a piece off each end to shorten the wires before making the closure.

❷ Follow the template on p. 18 to make the simple hook-and-eye clasp shown on the necklace on p. 18 or design a clasp of your own. The hook and eye have to be at right angles to each other to connect.

❸ Finish shaping the neckwires so they sit comfortably around your neck.

gemstone necklace

A twisted-wire coil encases the wire section of my lapis necklace. You can also cut the coils and intersperse them

with silver or other decorative beads.

❶ Cut a 14-in. (35cm) length of 14-gauge wire. Fold the twisted wire in half and place the core wire into the fold. Hold the twisted wire and core in one hand. With your other hand, wrap the twisted wire around the core, spacing the wraps evenly (**photo h**). When you reach the end, turn the piece around and continue wrapping with the reserved wire until you have a 12-in. (30cm) coil. Slide the completed coil off the core and set aside.

materials

both necklaces
- 18 in. (45cm) 14-gauge Sterling silver wire
- G-S Hypo Cement (optional)

Tools: round- and chainnose pliers, metal file, wire cutters

pearl necklace
- 5 in. (13cm) of 7mm Freshwater pearls
- Medium-weight silk or nylon beading cord
- 4 6mm Round sterling silver large-hole beads
- 2 6mm Round sterling silver small-hole beads
- Twisted wire beading needles

Tools: awl or similar knotting aid

gemstone necklace
- 6 in. (15cm) of Gemstone beads
- 12 Small square silver spacers
- 4 6mm Round sterling silver large-hole beads
- 12 ft. (3.6m) 24-gauge Sterling silver twisted wire
- Flexible beading wire, size .013 or .014
- Crimp beads

Tools: crimping pliers

h

i

❷ Cut the 14-gauge wire in half. Turn small loops on these wires as previously described.

❸ String a crimp bead onto 10 in. (25cm) of flexible beading wire, go through a loop on a neckwire, then back through the crimp bead, leaving a 1 in. (2.5cm) tail. Push the crimp close to the wire loop and crimp it (see "Basics").

❹ String 6 in. of gemstones and spacers, ending with a gemstone. String a crimp bead. Go through the loop on the other neckwire and back through the crimp and a bead or two (**photo i**). Tighten the strand and crimp.

❺ String 2 large-hole silver beads on each neckwire. The first bead slides over the loop to hide the crimp. The second sits against the first to cover the exposed loop.

❻ Cut the 12-in. twisted wire coil in half and string one half on each neckwire. You'll need about 1-1½ in. (2.5-3.8cm) of exposed core to make the clasp, so trim the coils, if necessary. Finish this necklace following the clasp and shaping directions given on p. 91. ❍—*M.B.*

Half-round Roman ring

*Create an elegant ring
with a flat bead and wire*

W ho doesn't like
rings? When I
spotted an ancient-
looking ring made with a
new tabular eye bead and a
bit of gold wire, it was lust at
first sight.

This style of ring can be
made with a round bead, but
it's much more comfortable
to wear if the bead has a flat
side to sit against your finger.
The bead also needs to have
a hole large enough to
accommodate 18- or 16-
gauge wire. Newer agates
are a better bet as a result,
since the older ones usually
have tiny holes in the center.

When I went through my
bead stash, I found a pretty
piece of Tibetan turquoise
(which offers protection
against falling) that had a
large enough hole. Another
candidate—excellent for a
more contemporary look—
was a furnace glass bead, a
blown-glass tube that also
features a hole big enough to
work well.

In a friend's stash, I finally
found my top choice: a perfect, flat-bottomed, tabular
eye bead (the carnelian ring
above right). For thousands
of years, many cultures have
believed that eye beads,
which are made from ringed
agates, ward off evil.

One can always use a little
extra protection.

stepbystep

❶ Center the bead on the
wire and use chainnose pliers
to bend the wire ends down
at a right angle ⅛-³⁄₁₆ in. (3-
5mm) beyond the bead on
both sides (**photo a**). (If you
are making the ring with a
very large-holed bead, string
a spacer bead on each side of
the main bead so it won't
slide over the wraps.)

❷ Wrap the wire ends
loosely around a mandrel
form, or use the widest
knuckle of the finger on which
you wish to wear the ring
(**photo b**). The wires should lie
next to each other and extend
past both sides of the bead.

❸ Cut the tails to about an
inch (2.5cm) past the bend.
Grasp the two wires adjacent
to a bend with flatnose pliers.
Using chainnose pliers, bend
the wire tail at a right angle
across the wire going through
the bead (**photo c**). Wrap the
tail around the wire that goes
through the bead, working
from the bend toward the
bead (**photo d**).

❹ Repeat on the other side
with the same number of
wraps. Trim the tails flush
and file away any burrs or
rough edges as necessary.

❺ Harden the wire a bit by
mashing the paired wire
band with your chainnose
pliers (**photo e**). ❍—*A.K.*

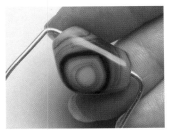

a

c

b

d

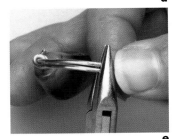

e

materials

- Flat-bottom bead about the
  width of your finger with a
  large hole (mine is from
  Kamol, 206-764-7375)
- 12 in. (25-30cm) 16- or
  18-gauge Sterling or gold-
  filled wire
- 2 Spacer beads (optional if
  using a bead with large hole

Tools: flat- and chainnose
pliers, wire cutter; ring mandrel
or form the circumference of a
ring that fits your finger

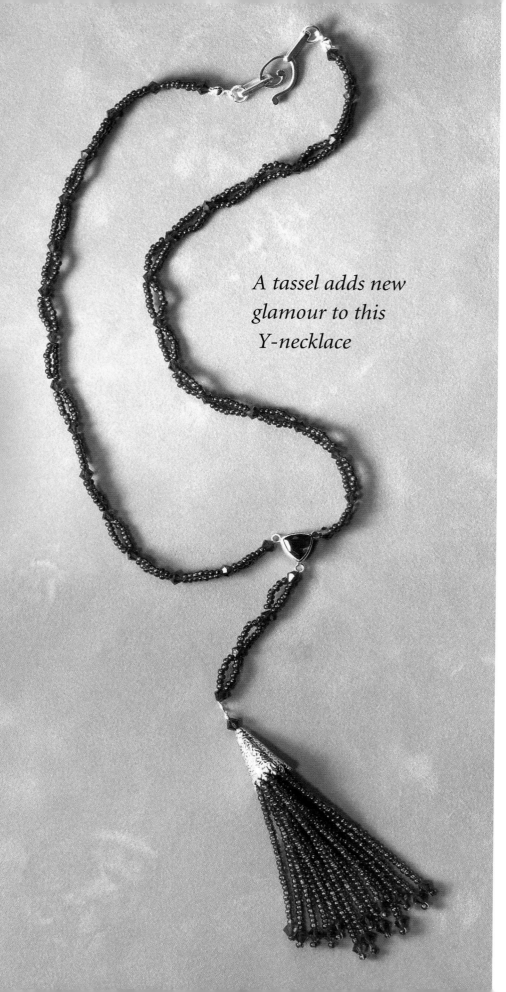

A tassel adds new glamour to this Y-necklace

Wonder

In the movies, the Y-necklace comes in and out of popularity. This rendition, however, transcends trends. Inspired by the trim, 3-loop garnet finding, I used a few crystals and a hank of 11º seed beads to complete the design.

stepbystep

making the tassel

❶ Thread a needle with 2 yd. (1.8m) of Fireline.

❷ String 2 in. (5cm) of seed beads, a crystal, and a seed bead. Leave a 4-in. (10cm) tail.

❸ Skip the last seed bead and sew back through the crystal and the remaining seed beads. Trim the thread, leaving a 4-in. tail. Tape the tail ends to secure the beads.

❹ Repeat steps 2-3 until you have made enough fringe to fill your cone. My tassel has 14 strands of fringe.

❺ Remove the tape from the fringe ends and gather the threads together, pushing the beads down so they are snug. Tie the ends into a loose overhand knot (see "Basics," p. 136). Tighten the knot firmly against the beads (**photo a**).

❻ Make a small wrapped loop at one end of the 3-in. (7.6 cm) piece of wire (see "Basics").

❼ Slip half the thread ends through the loop and tie the ends around the loop using a square knot (**photo b**). Glue the knot and trim the ends to ¼ in. (6mm).

❽ Insert the wire into the wide end of the cone and pull the knotted ends into the cone (**photo c**).

❾ String a crystal onto the wire and make a wrapped loop above it (**photo d**).

stringing the necklace

1 Measure your neckline to determine the necklace's length without the tassel.

2 Cut 1 yd. (.9m) of Fireline and thread a needle on each end.

3 Take one needle through a side loop on the 3-loop finding and center the finding on the thread.

4 Sew both needles through a crystal and push it against the loop, keeping the finding centered on the thread.

5 String 7 seed beads and a crystal on one needle and slide them down to the first crystal strung.

6 String 7 seed beads on the other needle and sew through the crystal strung in step 5 (**photo e**).

7 Repeat steps 5-6 until the length is within ½ in. (1.3cm) of half the desired necklace length.

8 Sew both needles into a bead tip. String a seed bead on one needle and tie the thread ends into a surgeon's knot (see "Basics" and **photo f**). Glue the knot and trim the threads. Close the bead tip and roll the hook over one end of the clasp.

9 Repeat steps 2-8 to string the other side of the necklace.

attaching the tassel

1 Repeat step 2 of "stringing the necklace" and take one needle through the wrapped loop at the top of the tassel. Center the loop on the thread.

2 Sew both needles through one crystal and push it against the loop, keeping the loop centered on the thread.

3 Repeat steps 5-6 of "stringing the necklace" three times.

4 Sew through the finding's available loop in opposite directions (**photo g**). Sew back through the last crystal strung and several of the beads, exiting between two seed beads.

5 Tie a front-back-front knot (see "Basics"), leaving the needles threaded (**photo h**). Glue the knot.

6 Sew through the beads toward the tassel and tie another front-back-front knot. Glue the knot and sew through a few more beads before trimming the threads close to the beads. ●—*P.O.*

a

b

c

d

e

f

g

h

materials

- **1** Hank 11º seed beads
- **50-60** 4mm Bicone crystals
- **1** 3-loop Finding
- **1** Clasp
- **1** Cone
- Fireline fishing line, 6 lb. test (available where fishing supplies are sold)
- Beading needles, #12
- **2** Bead tips
- G-S Hypo cement
- 3 in. (7.6cm) 22-gauge Sterling silver wire, half-hard

Tools: chain- and roundnose pliers, diagonal wire cutters

d

e

f

g

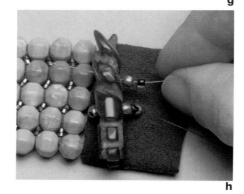

h

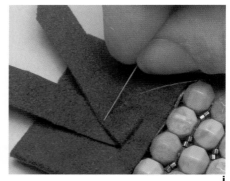

i

have completed the bead rows between the loom's coil spreaders, turn the take-up roller at the starting end to bring any beads beyond the coil spreader into the loom's working area. Continue weaving until all but the last row of stone beads has a row of cylinder beads woven after it.

12 Put the needle aside and repeat step 7 to weave a selvage at this end.

13 Pick up the needle again and sew through the edge bead on the last row of stone beads. Stitch through the edge of the selvage with the threaded needle, tying several half-hitch knots to secure the thread. Trim the thread.

finish the ends

1 Remove the work from the loom and lay it flat on your work surface.

2 Cut 2 pieces of Ultrasuede 1½ x 4 in. (3.8 x 10cm).

3 Center one piece of Ultrasuede under one of the selvages. Trim the warp and weft cord ends close to the woven selvage.

4 Coat the selvage with E6000 glue and allow it to seep through. Fold each side of the Ultrasuede over so they are even with the bracelet's sides and the edges overlap in the center (**photo f**). Press so that the glue adheres securely. Allow the glue to dry completely and trim the Ultrasuede so the edge is even.

5 Repeat steps 3-4 at the other end of the bracelet.

make the lashing

I chose an oblong bead with two holes for the closure. To secure it, I made a Y-shaped beaded shank. A single-hole oblong bead or button will only require a straightforward beaded shank.

1 Thread a needle with 1 yd. (.9m) of

Silamide and knot the end of the thread.

2 Sew through the center of one Ultrasuede panel, from the back to the front. Pick up a 2mm bead, a 6º seed bead, and a 2mm bead and go through one hole in the 2-hole bead. Pick up a 2mm bead and sew back through the beads and the Ultrasuede panel (**photo g**).

3 Sew back up through the Ultrasuede and through the first 2mm bead. Pick up a 6º seed bead and a 2mm bead and sew through the other hole in the 2-hole bead (**photo h**). Pick up a 2mm bead and sew back through the beads and the Ultrasuede.

4 Sew through the beads two or three more times to secure the oblong bead.

5 Cut a strip of Ultrasuede 7½-in. long and ¼-in. (19cm x 6mm) wide. Trim the ends at an angle. Make a slightly off-center fold about 1½ in. (3.8cm) from one end and position the fold in the center of the Ultrasuede panel at the bracelet's other end.

6 Sew the strip to the panel by stitching across the lashing strip about ¼ in. from the folded edge (**photo i**). Sew across it again to secure. You can also embellish the seam with a line of cylinder beads.

wearing the bracelet

To wear the bracelet, wrap the lashing strip around the shank of the 2-hole bead 3 or 4 times. To keep it secure, thread the strip's end back under itself and pull tight. If you have difficulty with the lashing remaining closed, sew a hook and eye to the bracelet's ends for extra security. ●—*P.O.*

Pearl ribbons

String pearls and small beads on chain

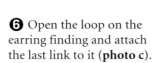

The secret to these bead ribbons is pairing different sizes of beads on chain with head pins. Try making these earrings with two sizes of crystals for a sparkling, dressy effect or with stone chips and seed beads for a casual look.

step by step

pink pearl ribbons

❶ Working near the tip of your chainnose pliers, bend the end of the wire into a hook. Then mash the hook closed side to side (**photo a**).

❷ String a crystal on the wire and go through the first link on one chain length. String a pearl on the wire and cut it about ⅛ in. (3mm) past the pearl.

❸ Bend the wire end into a hook with the tip of the pliers (**photo b**). Then mash the hook closed.

❹ Repeat steps 2-3 on the third link and every other link, lining up the crystals on the same side of the chain.

❺ When you've strung 11 pins, cut the chain, leaving 2 plain links above the last pin.

❻ Open the loop on the earring finding and attach the last link to it (**photo c**).

champagne earrings

❶ Form these earrings like the pink ones but string a 2-cut seed bead instead of the crystal.

❷ Insert a pin through every link and reverse the order of the beads on every other pin (**photo d**).

❸ Attach the earring finding to the sixteenth link.

double ribbons

❶ Form the pins for these earrings as above with a charlotte on one end and a pearl on the other.

❷ Insert 12 pins, one through every other link, alternating seeds and pearls on each side.

❸ Skip 4 links. Then place 10 more pins on every other link, alternating seeds and pearls. Cut off the chain after the last pin (**photo e**).

❹ Attach the earring finding to the third link after the twelfth pin (**photo f**). ●—A.K.

a

b

c

d

f

e

materials

pink pearl ribbon
- **2** 23-link Lengths of 2.5mm gold-filled cable chain
- **22** 3.5mm Pink pearls
- **22** 3mm Swarovski crystals
- **1** Pair gold-filled French hook earring findings
- 18-24 in. (46-61cm) 24-gauge Gold-filled wire, dead soft

champagne ribbons
- **2** 16-link Lengths of 2.2mm cable chain
- **30** 3mm Champagne pearls
- **30** 2-cut Seed beads, size 12º, bronze color
- **1** Pair post earring findings with a loop
- 24-30 in. (61-76cm) 24-gauge Gold-filled wire, dead soft, or **8-10** gold-filled ultra-thin head pins (Beadworld, 206-523-0530)

double ribbons
- **2** 47-link Lengths of 2.5mm silver cable chain
- **44** 3-3.5mm Flat keshi pearls
- **44** Charlotte seed beads, size 11º
- 36 in. (.9m) 24-gauge Sterling silver wire, dead soft, or **10-12** ultra-thin head pins
- **1** Pair earring findings with a loop

Tools: chainnose pliers and diagonal wire cutters

Contemporary accents

Highlight a multi-strand necklace with art glass beads

W hen an editor of one of *Bead&Button*'s sister publications came to work wearing a lovely, multi-strand necklace, we were curious about its origin. The piece turned out to be one of her own designs, and we knew we had another bead enthusiast in our midst.

stepbystep

Stringing on doubled cord is one of the basic techniques of jewelry-making, but sometimes it's necessary to break the rules. I used a single cord for each strand in this necklace, so the knotted ends would fit easily into the unusual clasp. If you'd rather finish the necklace using a conventional clasp, follow the directions on p. 120 for using head pins (or wire) and cones to hide the knotted ends, then attach your clasp.

❶ Determine the finished length of your necklace. Mine is 16 in. (41cm) including a 1⅜-in. (3.4cm) clasp. To lengthen or shorten the necklace, adjust the length of the beaded sections on each side of the clasp.

❷ Cut nine 40-in. (1m) lengths of beading cord. Working with one cord at a time, fold each cord in half and attach it to a clasp spring with a lark's head knot (see "Basics," p. 136 and **photo a**).

❸ Cut (never pull) one strand from a hank and transfer 3 in. (7.6m) of beads to one of the 18 cords (**photo b**). Add a few crystals to this beaded strand, if desired, and secure the beads with a small piece of tape. Repeat with the remaining cords, keeping the crystals sparse and randomly spaced. If you're using more than one bead color, divide the colors among the strands.

❹ Remove the tape and string a spacer, an accent bead, and a spacer onto all the cords (**photo c**). The spacer prevents the seed beads from slipping into the art bead.

❺ String the next 3 beaded sections as in steps 3 and 4, but make each of these sections 2-in. (5cm) long. For the last (fifth) section, string 3 in. of beads as at the start.

a

b

c

d

e

❻ Check your work to make sure that the strands are even and untangled before finishing the necklace. Select any 2 strands from the group and tie them together with the first half of a surgeon's knot (see "Basics"). Allow a little ease in each strand. Then finish the surgeon's knot, working over the remaining spring (**photo d**). Tie another surgeon's knot for additional security. Don't trim the excess cord.

❼ Repeat step 6 with the remaining cords. Glue the knots and let dry. Trim the tails about ⅜ in. (1cm) past the knot. Glue the tails together so they point away from the necklace (**photo e**). Let the glue dry.

❽ Insert each spring into a clasp half as shown in **photo f**. If the spring does not go into the clasp easily, grab the wire loop with chainnose pliers and push it gently until it locks in place. ●—*M.B.*

materials

- **3** Hanks seed beads, size 12º one-cuts, 1 or more colors
- **4** Art glass or other accent beads, approximately 14 x 20mm (these are by Jennifer Wilson through Eclectica, p. 67)
- **8** Small spacers (hole must be large enough to accommodate 18 strands of beading cord)
- **50** 3mm Crystals (optional)
- Fireline fishing line, 6 lb. test or thin nylon beading cord
- Twisted wire needles
- Clasp—sterling bead/chain ends with spring (Rio Grande 800-545-6566)
- G-S Hypo Cement

Tools: chainnose pliers

f

Liquid silver
jewelry ensemble

Create a waterfall of shimmering silver over semi-precious stones

Liquid silver beads are thin tubes of sterling silver that drape elegantly when strung en masse. The tubes come in various lengths and diameters and can be either straight or twisted. For these pieces, I chose the finest diameter of straight tubes in a 2mm length. The tubes are so fine that it takes many strands to make a necklace that doesn't look skimpy. If you decide to use slightly fatter tubes, you may not need quite as many strands.

stepbystep

Start the necklace by making three 5-bead spacer bars. Then string the strands in groups, starting with the inner and outer sets. As you work with each group of cords, wind the ones you aren't using on a card to help prevent the multiplicity of cords and needles from tangling. After completing the strands, attach the cones and clasp. When you string the bracelet and earrings, work with a few strands at a time to avoid tangling.

spacer bars

❶ Cut an 18-in. (46cm) length of size 1 bead cord and thread a twisted wire needle on each end.

❷ String 2 seed beads to the center of the cord. Then pass both needles through a stone bead. String a seed bead on each needle and pass both needles through another stone bead. Lay one needle aside.

❸ On the second needle string 1 seed bead and 1 stone bead 3 times. Then string 2 seed beads and go back through

the last stone bead toward the start (**photo a**).

❹ String a seed bead and go through the next stone bead. Repeat. End by stringing a final seed bead. The needles now meet at the second stone bead strung. Tighten the cords so the seed beads lie in pairs and there is no slack. Tie the two cords together with a surgeon's knot (see "Basics," p. 136 and **photo b**).

❺ Bring both cords through the second stone bead and tie another surgeon's knot. Go through the seed beads and the first stone bead and clip the cords. Glue the knots.

❻ Make two more spacer bars.

silver strands

This necklace consists of six groups of liquid silver strands. Begin each group with 4 strands of silver strung on doubled cord. After passing through the first spacer bar, string the cords as singles. Continue stringing on single cords through the second spacer bar. (Both front necklace sections consist of 8 strands of silver per group.) String on doubled cord again after the third spacer bar, so the design repeats its 4-strand start.

❶ Cut four 2-yd. (1.8m) lengths of beading cord and string a needle to the center of each. Tie the tails together temporarily with a slip knot about 4-6 in. (10-15cm) from the ends. Keep the needles and cords from tangling.

❷ For group 1, the innermost strands, string 5 in. (13cm) of liquid silver on each doubled strand and thread each through the tiny space between the

paired seed beads on one end of a spacer bar. Be careful not to split the threads.

❸ For group 6, the outermost strands, repeat steps 1-2, stringing 6¼ in. (16cm) of silver and passing through the space between the beads at the opposite end of the spacer bar (**photo c**).

❹ Slide the needles in group 1 away from the center of the cords and cut the cords at the fold. Set aside the 4 strands without needles.

❺ String 4 in. (10cm) of liquid silver on the strands with needles and go through a second spacer bar, as in step 2.

❻ Set these strands aside, thread needles on the other 4 cords, and repeat step 5 with them.

❼ Repeat steps 5-6 to make the next section of the necklace. Take all 8 strands through the end space on the third spacer bar.

❽ Remove 4 needles from these strands and double-up with the

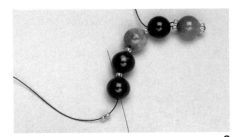

a

b

c

e

f

g

materials

- **2 oz.** Liquid silver beads
- **25** Twisted wire beading needles
- **1** Spool Nylon bead cord, size 0, Silamide, Kevlar bead thread, or Fireline 6 lb. test

Tools: round- and chainnose pliers, wire cutter

necklace

- **15** 6mm Moss agate beads
- **36** Seed beads, size 11°
- **2 yd.** (1.8m) Nylon bead cord, size 1
- **2** 1¾-in. (4.5cm) Curved sterling silver cones
- **10 in.** (25cm) 20- or 22-gauge Sterling silver wire, half hard or dead soft
- **2-4** 3-4mm Sterling silver beads
- **1** Sterling silver toggle clasp

bracelet

- **2** ¾-in. (7cm) Straight sterling silver cones
- **6 in.** (15cm) 20- or 22-gauge Sterling silver wire
- **2-4** 3-4mm Sterling silver beads
- **1** Sterling silver toggle clasp

earrings

- **2** ¾-in. Straight sterling silver cones
- **6 in.** (15cm) 20- or 22-gauge Sterling silver wire
- **2** 3-4mm Sterling silver beads
- **1** Pair earring findings with a loop

remaining needles to create 4 doubled cords. Repeat step 2.

9 Tighten the beads and tie the strands together temporarily with another slip knot.

10 Repeat steps 4-9 with the cords in group 6, stringing 6½ in. (17cm) of silver on the center sections (**photo d**).

11 Repeat these steps for groups 2-5 with these changes:

Group 2—string 5¼ in. (13.3cm) on the 4-strand (back) sections and 4½ in. (11.4cm) on the 8-strand (front) sections.

Group 3—string 5½ in. (14cm) on the 4-strand sections and 5 in. (12.7cm) on the 8-strand sections.

Group 4—string 5¾ in. (14.6cm) on the 4-strand sections and 5½ in. (14cm) on the 8-strand sections.

Group 5—string 6 in. (15.2cm) on the 4-strand sections and 6 in. on the 8-strand sections.

12 To finish the necklace, make sure the beads are snug, divide the 6 groups in half, and tie the two together with overhand knots (see "Basics") just past the end beads.

13 Cut the 10-in. length of wire into two equal pieces and make a wrapped

loop (see "Basics") that will fit up into the curved cone. Pass one bunch of threads through the loop from back to front and the other through in the opposite direction (**photo e**). Then tie a front-back-front knot around the wire (see "Basics"). End with a final square knot (**photo f**). Glue the knots. When the glue is dry, trim the tails, leaving about ⅛ in. (3mm). Repeat on the other end of the necklace.

14 Pull each wire through a cone to hide the knots. String a 3-4mm bead on the wire at the top of each cone and begin a wrapped loop. Pull the loop end of the clasp into one of the wire loops and finish the wrap. If the bar end of the clasp does not have a chain, string 2-3 silver beads on the cone wire before attaching the bar part of the clasp to it.

bracelet

1 String the bracelet with 24 strands of liquid silver, using Fireline in single

strands or doubled nylon cord. The strands of liquid silver should be the desired finished length of the bracelet minus the length of the cones and the clasp.

2 Divide the strands into two bunches of 12 each and finish as in steps 13-14.

earrings

1 For each earring, string ten 3-in.- (7.6cm) long strands on 10-in. (25cm) cords. Tie the strands together with an overhand knot at each end of the silver, leaving a tiny amount of slack so the strands drape well.

2 Make a wrapped loop that will fit inside a cone on one end of a 3-in. piece of wire. Then pass one bundle of strands through the loop in one direction and the other through in the other direction and tie them together with a surgeon's knot (**photo g**). Glue securely before cutting off the tails.

3 Pull the wire into a cone, string a 3mm silver bead, and make a small wrapped loop above it. Attach the earring finding to the loop.

4 Make the second earring. **●**—*A.K*

Simply linked

A few beads and bits of chain make versatile bracelets

This easy bracelet design can feature one gorgeous bead or an assortment. Just string your centerpiece on half-hard wire or flexible beading wire and attach it to the chain. Almost any kind of clasp will work—toggle, magnetic, or lobster. Each bracelet above uses a different closure.

stepbystep

wire centerpiece

❶ Measure your wrist. Add 1 in. (2.5cm) for ease. Divide the length by 3. The beaded centerpiece will be one third of the length, and the chain and clasp will be two thirds.

❷ Add 2 in. (5cm) to the one-third measurement. Cut a piece of wire this length. To make the double-wire centerpiece, cut two pieces.

❸ Measure your clasp's length and subtract it from the two-thirds measurement. Cut a piece of chain this length, then cut it in half (**photo a**).

❹ Make a right-angle bend in the wire ¾ in. (1.9cm) from an end. Start a wrapped loop (see "Basics," p.136) and insert an end link of one piece of chain into the loop before wrapping it (**photo b**).

❺ String the beads on the wire until the beaded length reaches the one-third measurement. Start a wrapped loop at this end of the wire and string an end link of the second piece of chain into the loop before wrapping it.

❻ If you are making the double-wire centerpiece, repeat steps 4-5 with the second piece of wire.

❼ Attach a split ring to each end of the chain. Attach one side of the clasp to each split ring. If you are using a lobster claw clasp, attach the claw to one end and use the split ring at the other end for the closure.

flexible beading wire centerpiece

❶ Repeat step 1 above.

materials

wire centerpiece
- **3-5** Stone beads or 6-8 in. (15-20cm) of stone chips
- **5-6 in. (12.7-15cm)** Chain
- **4-5 in. (10-12.7cm)** 22-gauge Half-hard wire, sterling silver or gold-filled (8-10 in./20-25cm for double-wire bracelet)
- **1** Clasp

flexible wire centerpiece
- **1** 2-3 in. (5-7.5cm) Oblong bead
- **4-5 in.** Flexible beading wire, 0.019
- **5-6 in.** Chain
- **1** Clasp
- **2** Crimp beads

Tools: diagonal wire cutters, chain- and roundnose pliers, crimping pliers

❷ Add 4 in. (10cm) to the one-third measurement. Cut a piece of flexible beading wire this length.

❷ Repeat step 3 above.

❸ String a crimp onto the wire. Thread 2 in. of the wire through the last link on one piece of chain and back through the crimp. Tighten the loop and crimp (**photo c**).

❹ String beads onto the wire and over the tail until the beaded length measures one third the bracelet's full length.

❺ String a crimp onto the wire and thread the wire

a

b

c

d

through the last link on the other piece of chain and back through the crimp and one or more beads. Tighten the loop and crimp. Trim the excess wire (**photo d**).

❻ To attach the clasp, repeat step 7 above. ●—*P.O.*

Understated elegance

String an easy two-hole pearl collar

As soon as I saw these two-hole pearls at my local bead store, I had to buy a strand. I knew I'd find something wonderful to do with them. Two-hole pearls are uncommon and somewhat costly, but they are lovely. You can use two-hole glass beads for an equally simple but elegant necklace. If you buy the pearls, you'll have enough left over to make a matching bracelet.

stepbystep

necklace

1 Put 1 square silver bead on a head pin. Thread the head pin through the middle hole of a 1-to-3 spreader and out the hole at the top. Thread on another square bead and turn a very small loop above it. Use chainnose pliers to mash the loop's sides together (**photo a**). The loop and bead need to fit inside an 8mm bead. Repeat with the other spreader.

2 Thread 2 twisted wire needles with 60 in. (1.5m) of cord. Center the needles and double the threads. Tie all four ends together in a fat overhand knot (see "Basics," p. 136). Glue the knot and trim the tails when dry.

3 Thread both needles through a bead tip (see "Basics"). Then thread them both through an 8mm silver bead.

4 Pass each needle through the top of a spreader between the square bead and the hole's edge (**photo b**). Bring one needle out each end hole. Press the 8mm bead onto the square bead (**photo c**). Then string a square bead on each pair of cords (**photo d**).

5 To contour the necklace, string fewer spacer beads between the inner pearl holes than between the outer holes. Don't confuse the cords.

6 From the end to the center, string the inner strand as follows: pearl, 1 seed bead (repeat for 12 seed beads); pearl, 2 seeds (3 times). String a pearl, 3 seeds, pearl, 2 seeds (2 times); repeat twice. End the first half with a pearl and 3 seeds.

7 Now you are at the center of the necklace. String a pearl and 2 seeds. Then repeat step 6 in reverse.

8 For the first half of the outer strand, string as follows, going through the bottom holes on the pearls: pearl, 2 seeds, pearl, 1 seed (6 times).

9 For the center front, go through the bottom hole of the next pearl and string a teardrop (21 times). Then go through the bottom hole of the next pearl and repeat step 8 in reverse.

10 End by stringing a square silver bead on each cord and going through the end holes on the other spreader. Work each needle out between the edge of the top hole and the square bead. String both needles through an 8mm bead and push it onto the square bead, as in step 4.

materials

necklace — 18 in. (45.7cm) including clasp
- **1** 16-in. (41cm) Strand 6 x 14mm two-hole pearls or glass beads (Eclectica, 262- 641-0910)
- **1** 16-in. Strand 4 x 6mm top-drilled teardrop pearls
- **3g** Seed beads, size 11º
- **1** Pair 3-to-1 16mm sterling silver triangular spreaders (dabeadbabe.com)
- **8** 2.5mm Square sterling silver beads
- **2** 8mm Round sterling silver beads
- **2** Sterling silver bead tips
- **1** Clasp
- **2** Head pins

bracelet
- Leftover pearls from necklace
- Leftover seed beads from necklace
- **1** Pair 3-to-1 16mm sterling silver triangular spreaders
- **8** 2.5mm Square sterling silver beads
- **2** 8mm Round sterling silver beads
- **2** Sterling silver bead tips
- **1** Magnetic clasp
- **2** Head pins

both
- Bitchin' Beads or Power Pro bead cord, size .006
- Twisted wire beading needles
- G-S Hypo Cement

Tools: chain- and roundnose pliers

11 String both needles into the second bead tip and string a seed bead on one needle. Remove any slack in the cords. Tie the cords together tightly over the seed bead with 1-2 surgeon's knots (see "Basics"). Glue the knot, and when dry, clip the cord. Press the halves of the bead tips closed with chainnose pliers.

12 With roundnose pliers, curl each bead tip hook around a loop on the clasp (**photo e**).

bracelet

1 Using 18-in. (46cm) lengths of doubled cord, begin the bracelet as in steps 1-4 of the necklace.

2 Both bracelet ends together measure 2½ in. (6.3cm). Add the length of the clasp and subtract this total from the desired finished length.

3 Depending on how many two-hole pearls are left, you can alternate pearls and teardrops on both edges or on one edge with 3 seed beads between pearls

a

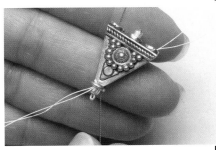

b

c

d

e

on the other edge. For a plainer bracelet, alternate pearls spaced with 1 or 2 seed beads on both edges.

4 End as in steps 10-12. ● *A.K.*

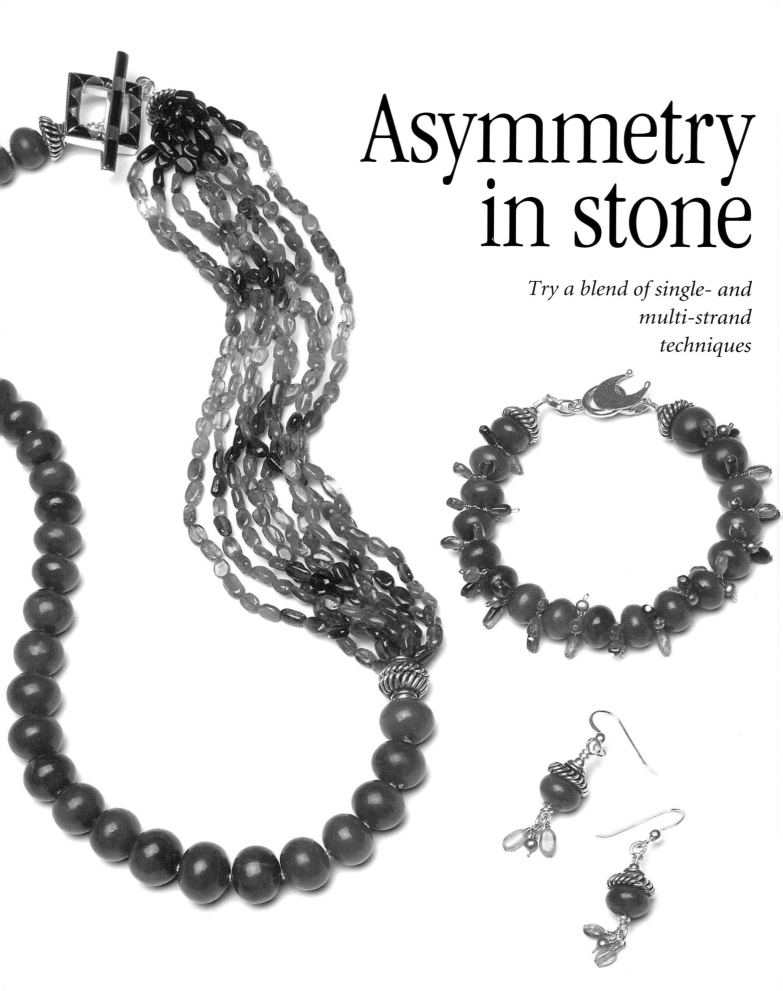

Asymmetry in stone

Try a blend of single- and multi-strand techniques

Multi-colored oval tourmaline beads are stunning but also stunningly expensive. As I was trying to figure out how I could afford to use them to make a multi-strand necklace that didn't look skimpy, it suddenly hit me that I would get a fuller effect if I shortened the length of the section where I planned to use the tourmalines in my design. That meant selecting another type of bead for more than half of my necklace—a challenge easily solved by a beautiful strand of coordinating dark green jade beads. I've used a pair of bead caps to hide the connection between the single- and multi-strand portions of this asymmetrical necklace. I've also designed a bracelet and earrings that use the leftover beads.

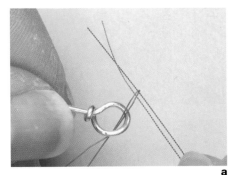

a

b

stepbystep

necklace

❶ Cut the wire into two 4-in. (10cm) lengths. Make a 4-6mm wrapped loop (see "Basics," p. 136) on each piece.

❷ For each tourmaline strand, cut a 30-in. (76cm) length of cord and thread a needle on each end. Fold the cord in half and put the folded end through one of the wrapped loops from back to front. Bring both needles through the folded cord (**photo a**). This is a lark's head knot (see "Basics"). String half a strand of tourmaline over both needles, one at a time (if the holes are very small) or held together. Start at the dark green end of the strand and keep the beads in order to preserve the color gradations.

❸ Take the needles through a bead cap, narrow end first, tighten the beads, and tie the cords to a split ring with several surgeon's knots (see "Basics" and **photo b**). Glue the knot and trim the cords ⅛ in. (3mm) past the knot.

❹ Repeat steps 2 and 3 for nine strands.

❺ Cut a 36-in. (.9m) cord. Thread a needle on each end and attach the cord to the second wrapped loop with a lark's head knot, as before. Alternate silver

spacers and jade beads for a length of 12-13 in. (30-33cm), starting and ending with a stone bead.

❻ String through a second bead cap, narrow end first, and through the ring attached to the tourmaline strands. Come back through the same bead cap and the first stone bead (**photo c**).

❼ Tighten the strand so the two bead caps meet, and glue them together (**photo d**).

❽ When the glued bead caps are dry, tie a front-back-front knot (see "Basics"). Go through a spacer and the next stone bead and tie another front-back-front knot. Repeat at least once more. End by going through two more beads and glue the knots.

❾ String a bead cap, wide end first, onto one of the wires at the end of the necklace. String one 3-4mm silver bead and start a medium-sized wrapped loop. Attach the ring end of the toggle clasp before completing the wrap (**photo e**).

❿ Repeat step 9 at the other end of the necklace, but string two 3-4mm silver beads between the bead cap and the wrapped loop that attaches the bar half of the clasp.

c

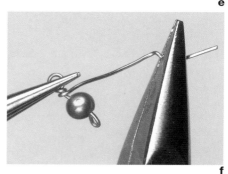

f

h

bracelet

❶ Cut a 2-in. (5cm) length of silver wire and bend the end into a hook with the tip of a chainnose pliers. Then mash the hook flat side-to-side (as in "Pearl Ribbons," p. 99). String a tourmaline or pearl on the wire and make a small wrapped loop above it (**photo f**). Repeat with all the remaining tourmalines and as many pearls as you have stone beads, or more.

❷ String a crimp on one end of the flexible beading wire. Take the end of the wire through a loop on the clasp and back through the crimp. Tighten the wire, leaving a small loop and a 1-in. (2.5cm) tail, and crimp (see "Basics").

❸ String a 3-4mm bead, then a bead cap, narrow end first, over both wires. String a stone bead and 1-3 dangles, alternating stones and dangles (**photo g**). Begin and end with a stone bead and finish with a bead cap and a 3-4mm bead. If the bracelet is long enough without two of the stone beads, reserve 4-6 dangles for matching earrings.

❹ String a crimp and the other end of the clasp. Go back through the crimp and several beads. Tighten the wire and crimp. Then cut off the tail.

earrings

❶ Cut the wire into two 4-in. lengths.

❷ Start a medium to large wrapped loop and string 2-3 dangles before completing the wrap. The loop should be big enough for the dangles to swing freely.

❸ String a stone bead then a bead cap, wide end first, and a 3-4mm silver bead. Start a small wrapped loop and attach it to the earring finding before completing the wrap (**photo h**).

❹ Make the second earring to match the first. ●—A.K.

materials

necklace
- **1** 18-in.(46cm) Strand graduated jade beads (Thunder Lizard, 505-751-1752)
- **5** 16-in. (41cm) Strands 5 x 4mm oval tourmaline beads
- **4** Sterling silver bead caps
- **8** in. (20cm) 18- or 20-gauge Sterling silver wire, dead soft
- Inlaid square toggle clasp (Scottsdale Bead Supply, 480-945-5988)
- **1** 4.5-6mm Split ring or soldered jump ring
- **2** in. (5cm) Tiny Thai silver spacers (Kamol, 206-764-7375)
- **3** 3-4mm Sterling silver beads
- Fray-resistant bead cord: Fireline 6-10# test, Bitchin' Beads, or Power Pro .006
- Twisted wire beading needles
- G-S Hypo Cement

bracelet
- Half a strand of tourmaline
- Remaining 6-7 in. (15-18cm) of jade beads
- **30-40** 3-4mm Champagne, pink, or green freshwater pearls
- **14** in. (36cm) Flexible beading wire, .018 or .019
- **2** Silver bead caps
- **2** 3-4mm Silver beads
- **2** Silver crimp beads
- **1** Silver toggle clasp
- **2** yd. (1.8m) 24-gauge Sterling silver wire, dead soft, or ultra-thin head pins (Beadworld, 206-523-0530)

Tools: crimping pliers (optional)

earrings
- **1** Pair silver earring findings with loop
- **2** Jade beads
- **4-6** Tourmaline and pearl dangles
- **2** Silver bead caps
- **2** 3-4mm Silver beads
- **8** in. (20cm) 20-gauge Sterling silver wire

Tools: round- and chainnose pliers, wire cutters

Mix and match

Make your own earring findings and a wardrobe of changeable dangles

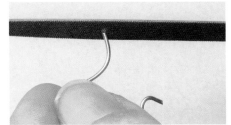

One package of earring wires can be used to finish five pairs of earrings that will be exactly the same at the top. When I realized this, I thought I might as well use the same two findings on each pair I made. What a thought! I decided to try my hand at making my own reusable findings. I'm so happy with the results that I'm planning a whole wardrobe of dangles to wear with them.

stepbystep

making an earring wire

❶ Cut two 3-in. (7.6cm) lengths of 20-gauge wire.

❷ Make a 90-degree bend about ⅜ in. (1cm) from one end of a wire.

❸ Using a ⅝-in.- (1.6cm) diameter dowel or a cylindrical object with a similar diameter (I used the top of a bottle of Liquid Paper), start at the bend made in step 2 and curve the wire three quarters of the way around the form (**photo a**). Allow the remaining wire to curve in the opposite direction.

❹ Remove the wire from the form without distorting the shape and trim the curved end of the wire with a straight cut so it measures approximately ¼ in. (6mm). Smooth this end of the wire with a file (**photo b**).

❺ Put a small dot of cyanoacrylate glue on the bent end of the wire. Insert this end in the hole of a half-drilled pearl (**photo c**). Remove any excess glue quickly and allow the bond to set.

❻ Repeat steps 2-5 with the second piece of wire.

❼ Make the dangles as described below. Slip the top loop or split ring onto the earring wire so it rests against the pearl.

making the purple dangles

❶ String a 7mm pearl, a Swarovski crystal spacer, a 5mm pearl, and a 3mm pearl on a headpin. Start a wrapped loop (see "Basics," p. 136) and insert the soldered jump ring before wrapping the loop (**photo d**).

❷ Repeat step 1 two more times, adding one more 3mm pearl to the top of the second dangle and two more 3mm pearls to the top of the third dangle.

❸ Repeat steps 1-3 for second dangle.

making the hippo dangles

❶ String a hippo charm, a spacer, a faceted rondelle, a spacer, and a 4mm oblong pearl on a head pin. Turn a wrapped loop above the pearl (**photo e**).

❷ Repeat step 1 to make a second dangle. ❍—*P.O.*

materials

- 6 in. (15.2cm) 20-gauge Wire
- **2** Half-drilled pearls (available from Rio Grande, 800-545-6566)
- Cyanoacrylate glue
- ⅝ in. (1.9cm) Diameter dowel or other cylindrical object
- **6** Swarovski crystal spacers
- **6** 7mm Pearls
- **6** 5mm Pearls
- **2** 4mm Pearls
- **12** 3mm Pearls
- **8** Head pins
- **2** Stone hippopotomus charms
- **4** Spacers, gold-filled
- **2** 6mm Faceted stone rondelles

Tools: chain- and roundnose pliers, diagonal wire cutters, file

Delicate dangle bracelets

Use slides to hang bead dangles on memory wire

Memory wire is perfect for making a wardrobe of fabulous bracelets. The coils stretch open, so the wire easily wraps around the wrist then stays in place. For a quick, easy approach, string assorted beads on a three-coil length of wire (see p. 60). Or use the special finding we show here—a sliding tube with a loop—to create a garden of dangling flowers and leaves on a single coil. For a more tailored look, work with stone or pearl bead dangles. The slides, which couldn't be easier to use, can be found in bead shops or ordered from a catalog of jewelry findings. Small and plain, they won't draw focus from the beads you dangle from them. Vary your effects by using one bead or a short cluster.

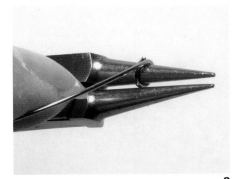

a

b

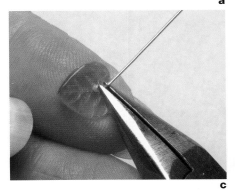

c

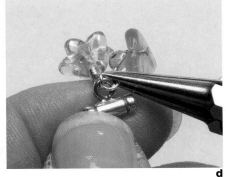

d

stepbystep

Never use jewelry cutters to cut memory wire. It will ruin them. Instead, grasp the wire with chainnose pliers where you want it to break and bend it back and forth until the wire weakens and snaps off. Begin the bracelet with a loop, string the slides and beads, and end with another loop. Then hang an extra dangle or group of dangles from each loop.

flower bracelet

❶ Break off a coil of memory wire long enough to go around your wrist, plus 1 in. (2.5cm), and turn a loop at one end. To turn a loop in memory wire, don't begin with a right-angle bend (as shown in "Basics," p. 136). Just start turning the loop. Make sure it is tightly closed or even turned a little past a full circle (**photo a**).

❷ For the dangles on the flower bracelet, string a faceted bead then a flower on a head pin and begin a wrapped loop above the flower. Hang the unwrapped loop on a slide finding before completing the wrap (**photo b**).

❸ Next, string a head pin through the hole at the top of a leaf bead from back to front and bend the head pin up at a right angle to the bead with a tiny space between the wire and the front of the

bead (**photo c**). String a green faceted bead on the wire so it nestles against the front of the leaf and begin a wrapped loop above it. Hook it onto the loop on the slide that already holds a flower and complete the wrap (**photo d**).

❹ Assemble 10-12 slides with dangles.

❺ Begin stringing the bracelet with a silver or pewter bead, then alternate slides and silver beads, ending with a silver bead ½-⅜ in. (1.3-1cm) from the end of the wire. You may need to assemble a few more slides.

❻ Make an over-turned loop at the end of the wire.

❼ Start 2 more flower dangles and 2 more leaf dangles and hang one of each from each loop on the bracelet ends before completing their wraps.

pearl bracelet

❶ Prepare the memory wire as in step 1 above.

❷ For each dangle, string a pearl on a head pin and begin a wrapped loop above the bead. Attach 1-3 dangles on each slide finding.

❸ String the bracelet. Begin and end with 1 glass bead, but put 2 between each slide. Finish with another over-turned loop.

❹ End by attaching one or more dangles to the end loops. ◐—A.K.

materials

flower bracelet

- Bracelet memory wire that goes around your wrist once plus 1 in. (2.5cm)
- 12-16 Silver slides with a loop (available from Rio Grande, 800-545-6566)
- 14-18 4mm Bali-style pewter or silver beads
- 14-18 5mm Bell-shaped flower beads
- 14-18 9mm Leaf beads with top hole
- 14-18 4mm Green fire-polished faceted beads
- 14-18 4mm Fire-polished faceted beads to match flowers
- 32-40 Silver head pins at least 1½ in. (3.8cm) long

crystal and pearl bracelet

- 10-14 Silver slides with a loop
- 20-28 4 x 6mm Faceted glass clear beads
- 12-16 Pearls for each of 3 sizes
- 36-48 Silver head pins at least 1½ in. (3.8cm) long, fine- or ultra fine-gauge for pearls

Tools: round- and chainnose pliers, wire cutters

A new look at foxtail

Try a professional stringing technique on chain

If you take apart an old necklace of metal or crystal beads, you may find that they were strung on thin chain rather than beading wire or cord. Not to be confused with "tigertail," a type of beading wire, this "foxtail" chain still offers a fast, practical way to securely string bulky or sharp-edged beads.

stepbystep

The sterling foxtail is woven and requires end crimps. The base metal foxtail has links that accept split rings.

crystal necklace

❶ Determine the finished length of your necklace. My necklace measures 19½ in. (48cm), including the clasp.

❷ Dab one end of the foxtail with glue and thread on an end crimp (**photo a**). Don't let the end of the foxtail extend beyond the crimp's cylinder.

❸ Use crimping pliers to squeeze the end crimp securely around the foxtail (**photo b**) (see "Basics," p. 136). Because an end crimp is longer than an ordinary crimp bead, you'll need to crimp twice to compress the cylinder's full length.

❹ String 3 in. (7.6cm) of spacers followed by a 12-in. (30cm) pattern of spacers and crystal beads. String another 3 in. of spacers and an end crimp.

❺ Dab glue onto the foxtail next to the last bead strung and move the end crimp over it. Crimp as in step 3. Trim the foxtail close to the crimp (**photo c**).

❻ Attach a split ring to each end crimp and the clasp to the split rings.

lapis lazuli necklace

❶ String the centerpiece bead and center in on the foxtail chain.

❷ String an alternating pattern of lapis and spacers on each side of the large bead until you reach the desired length.

❸ Slide a split ring through the pair of foxtail links at either end (**photo d**). You may need to widen the links slightly with a needle or push pin to insert the ring.

❹ Trim the unfinished chain to about ¼ in. (6mm) from the end bead and repeat step 3. Attach the clasp to the split rings. ❍—*M.B.*

materials

Foxtail has a larger diameter than most beading wires, so choose beads with adequate holes.

quartz crystal and sterling necklace

- 1 16-in. (40cm) Strand faceted quartz crystal beads
- **100-150** 2.5mm Sterling silver spacer beads
- 2 ft. (60cm) Sterling silver foxtail chain
- 2 End crimps
- 2 Sterling silver split rings
- Clasp
- G-S Hypo Cement or Zap-A-Gap Super Glue

Tools: split-ring opener, crimping pliers, diagonal wire cutters

lapis lazuli necklace

- 1 16-in. Strand stone beads
- 1 Pkg. (100 pieces) Bali silver spacers
- Centerpiece bead
- 2 ft. Base metal foxtail chain
- 2 Split rings
- Clasp

Tools: split-ring opener, diagonal wire cutters

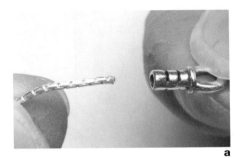
a

b

c

d

Falling leaves

String this pearl necklace with a crystal dangle centerpiece

The starting point for this glamorous necklace was a set of five vintage crystal leaf pendants. I was initially attracted by their deep olive green color. When I saw twinkling pink highlights, I was sold. After considering many color options for showing them off, I decided to stick with a verdant palette. I selected crystals, pearls, stones, and glass foil beads to echo the green gleam. As a result, those flashes of pink fire stand out even more.

step by step

Try different dangle combinations before you start assembling the necklace. I strung the beads on head pins, experimenting with different combinations before I settled on the final design.

make the dangles

❶ Cut 3½ in. (8.9cm) of 24-gauge wire. Curve the bottom 1½ in. (3.8cm) so the wire resembles a fish hook.

❷ String a leaf pendant on the wire so it rests at the bottom of the bend (**photo a**). Make a right-angle bend on the wire's short end about ⅛ in. (3mm) above the dangle so that it crosses the long wire end (**photo b**). Pull the long end so it slopes over the dangle and begin to wrap the short wire end around the long end. Wrap 2 or 3 times and trim the excess wire. Center the wrapped wire over the dangle (**photo c**).

❸ String a bicone crystal on the wire so it rests on the wire wrap. Make a wrapped loop (see "Basics," p. 136) above the crystal.

❹ Repeat steps 2-3 with the 4 remaining leaf pendants.

❺ Cut 2½ in. (6.4cm) of 24-gauge wire and make a wrapped loop at one end. String a gold spacer, a rondelle, a rectangular glass bead, a rondelle, and a gold spacer on the wire. Start a wrapped loop at the wire's other end and slip the loop of one of the assembled pendant dangles into it before closing the loop (**photo d**).

❻ Repeat step 5 twice to attach 2 more of the assembled pendant dangles.

❼ Cut 3 in. (7.6cm) of 24-gauge wire and make a wrapped loop at one end. String a gold spacer, a rondelle, and a pearl on the wire. Start a wrapped loop at the other end and slip the top loop of a two-part dangle made in steps 5-6 into the loop before wrapping it.

❽ Repeat step 7 twice and attach the two remaining single pendant dangles to the bottom loops before wrapping them.

❾ String a bicone crystal on a head pin and make a wrapped loop at the top (**photo e**). Repeat with the 5 remaining head pins.

❿ Repeat step 7 twice, attaching one of

materials

necklace
- **5** Leaf-shaped crystal dangles, 25 x 15mm (available at Eclectica, 262-641-0910)
- **3** Rectangular foiled glass beads, 12 x 10mm
- **1-2** 16-in. Strand(s) 8mm Oval pearls
- **11** 8 x 5mm Faceted smoky quartz rondelles
- **15** 4mm Disc-shaped beads, gold-filled
- **18** 8mm Bicone crystals
- **25** in. (64cm) Flexible beading wire, 0.019
- **55** in. (1.4m) 24-gauge Gold-filled wire
- **6** Head pins, gold filled
- **1** Clasp, gold-filled

earrings
- **8** 4mm Disc-shaped beads, gold-filled
- **2** 8mm Bicone crystals
- **2** 8mm Oval pearls
- **2** 8 x 5mm Faceted smoky quartz rondelles
- **2** Head pins, gold filled
- **2** Earring findings, gold filled

Tools: chain- and roundnose pliers, diagonal wire cutters, crimping pliers

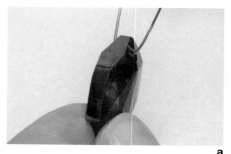

a

b

c

d

e

f

g

h

i

j

the bicone crystal dangles made in step 9 to the bottom loops (**photo f**).

⓫ Cut 2 in. of gold-filled wire and make a wrapped loop at one end. String a bicone crystal and start a wrapped loop at the other end. Slip the top of one of the 7 multi-part dangles into the wrapped loop before closing it. Repeat with 6 remaining multi-part dangles (**photo g**).

string the necklace

❶ Measure your neckline. You will want this necklace to be close to your neckline as the dangles are quite long. Add 5 in. (12.7cm) to your neckline length. Subtract the length of your clasp and cut a length of flexible beading wire to this measurement.

❷ String the four-part (or longest) leaf dangle to the center of the wire. String a pearl on each end of the wire.

❸ String one of the longer three-part leaf dangles onto each end of the wire (**photo h**). String a pearl after each one.

❹ String one of the shorter three-part leaf dangles onto each end of the wire (**photo i**). String a pearl after each one.

❺ String one of the two shortest dangles onto each end of the wire. String a pearl after each one.

❻ String a bicone crystal dangle, a pearl, and a bicone crystal dangle onto each end of the wire.

❼ String the same number of pearls on each side of the necklace until you reach the desired length determined in step 1.

❽ String 2 gold spacers, a crimp, and the loop of one end of the clasp onto the wire. Thread the wire end back through the crimp and the spacers. Crimp the crimp bead (see "Basics" and **photo j**) and trim the excess wire.

❾ Repeat step 8 at the other end of the necklace, adjusting the tension so the beads are snug before you crimp.

make the earrings

1. String a spacer, a bicone crystal, a spacer, a pearl, a spacer, a rondelle, and a spacer on head pin.
2. Make a wrapped loop above the beads.
3. Open the earring finding's bottom loop and slip in the wrapped loop before closing it.
4. Make a second earring to match the first. ●—*P. O.*

The personal touch

Trim a purchased handbag with bead embroidery

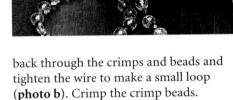

To embellish a store-bought purse with beads, choose a well-proportioned one with at least one plain surface for the beadwork. Choose a soft fabric for ease of embroidery.

stepbystep

❶ Enlarge or reduce the pattern in the **figure** to fit your purse and transfer the design to the bag's surface.

❷ Work in beaded backstitch over the solid lines (see "Basics," p. 136 and **photo a**).

❸ To add a beaded strap, remove the original and trim away any loose threads. Cut a piece of beading wire 4 in. (10cm) longer than the beaded strap's finished length.

❹ To make the strap removable, string a crimp bead, one or two accent beads, another crimp, and the clasp onto the beading wire. Take the beading wire back through the crimps and beads and tighten the wire to make a small loop (**photo b**). Crimp the crimp beads.

For a permanent strap, string a soldered jump ring instead of the clasp.

❺ String the beading wire to complement the embroidery. Avoid beads with sharp edges that might be uncomfortable to wear or hold.

❻ Finish the strap by stringing crimps, accent beads, and a clasp or jump ring, as in step 4. Go back through this sequence of beads, tighten the wire, and crimp as before.

❼ If you finished your strap with soldered jump rings, sew the rings to the bag where you removed the original strap.

If you used clasps on the strap, sew the soldered jump rings onto the bag where you removed the original strap (**photo c**). Then attach and remove the strap as the mood strikes. ❍—*M.B.*

a

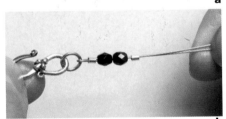

b

c

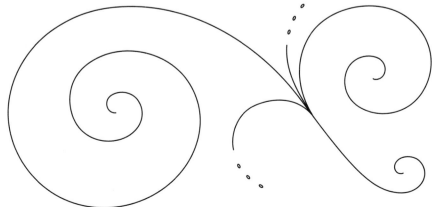

materials

- Fabric purse
- Seed beads (for embroidery)
- Assorted gemstones and crystals (for strap)
- Nymo D or Fireline fishing line 6 lb. test
- Beading needles, #10
- Transfer pens or paper (available at craft and fabric stores)
- Flexible beading wire .019
- **4** Crimp beads
- **2** S-hook or lobster claw clasps (optional)
- **2** 5mm soldered jump rings

Tools: crimping or chainnose pliers

Hooked on pearls

Combine decorative cones with an art bead for an elegant centerpiece

When Alice returned from the Tucson bead shows with these sterling silver pieces, I decided to create a necklace that would show off all three elements. I gathered the beaded strands into the cones as usual, but turned the closure from the back to the front to bring the cones and the art bead together in a cohesive overall design.

a

b

stepbystep

❶ Thread a twisted wire needle onto a 62-in. (1.5m) length of beading cord. Using the cord doubled, string 23 in. (58cm) of randomly spaced pearls and spacers. String 5 strands. (Set aside several pearls for finishing.) Select larger pearls for the ends of the strands to fill the cone openings. Leave at least 4-in. (10cm) tails for easy knotting.

❷ Working one end of the necklace at a time, tie the strands together with an overhand knot (see "Basics," p. 136) close to the end beads.

❸ Cut two 3-in. (7.6cm) pieces of 20-gauge wire (if you're using wire instead of head pins). Make a small wrapped loop (see "Basics") at one end of the wires or head pins. Tie each knotted group of strands to a loop with a surgeon's knot (see "Basics" and **photo a**). Glue the knots and trim the extra cord.

❹ Insert the straight end of the head pin or wire through the cone's wide opening so the loop and knots are hidden inside (**photo b**). Make a small wrapped loop close to the opening (**photo c**). Repeat with the other wire and cone.

❺ String the art bead on the remaining piece of 20-gauge wire. Make a wrapped loop on each end of the wire close to the bead (**photo d**).

❻ If you've designed your necklace to go over your head (no clasp), link the 2 cones and art bead with wrapped loop connectors, as follows: Center a pearl on a 3-in. piece of 24-gauge wire or head pin. Make the first half of a wrapped loop on each side of the pearl, working as close to the pearl as you can. Slide one partial loop through the wrapped loop on a cone and the other partial loop through one end of the art bead (**photo e**). Complete the wraps. Repeat to attach the other cone to the art bead.

materials

24-in. (60cm) finished length

- **6-7** 16-in. (40cm) Strands 4-7mm freshwater pearls in assorted shapes or a bead mixture
- **300** 2mm Sterling silver spacer beads or size 11º seed beads
- **2** Decorative sterling silver cones
- Art bead (Scottsdale Bead Supply (480) 945-5988)
- Nylon beading cord (such as Stringth, PowerPro, or Fireline 6lb. test)
- Twisted wire needles
- 12 in. (30cm) 20-gauge Dead-soft sterling silver wire (or **2** 18-gauge head pins, and 6 in./15cm of wire)
- 6 in. (15cm) 24-gauge Half-hard sterling silver wire and **1** 24-gauge head pin or **3** 24-gauge head pins
- **Tools:** round- and chainnose pliers, wire cutters

c

d

❼ To make a simple front clasp, adapt the connectors to include a small hook. Bend ¾ in. (2cm) of the wire piece into a tight "U," so the shorter segment lines up next to the longer one (**photo f, bottom**). Then fold the doubled section in half, forming a small hook. Slide a pearl onto the straight end of the wire and make half of a wrapped loop close to the pearl (**photo f, upper left**). Connect the partial loop to a loop on the art bead and finish the wraps.

To make the second connector, elongate one loop so it is the same length as the hook (**photo f, top right**). Connect the elongated loop to the cone and the other loop to the art bead. Complete the wraps.

❽ Add a dangle below the art bead by stringing a pearl on a head pin. Make thew first half of a wrapped loop above the pearl and attach the partial loop to the art bead. Complete the wrapped loop. ◗—*M.B.*

e

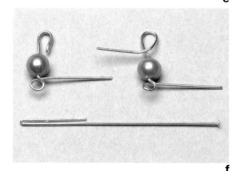

f

Appliqué cuff

Wrap your wrist with unusual stones

To get the proper shape for your leather cuff, start with a cylinder the circumference of the bracelet you want to make. I suggest that you measure the jars and bottles in your kitchen cabinets until you find one the right size. Mine turned out to be the onion powder bottle. To make the sewing easy, appliqué the beads onto a single loose layer of leather or Ultrasuede. Glue the appliquéd piece to the stiffened bracelet form, then line it with another clean leather piece. Those neat tricks make this bracelet much easier to construct than anyone would guess.

step by step

bracelet form

❶ Cut 1 piece of Ultrasuede twice the width of your bracelet plus ¼ in. (6mm) and the desired length (your wrist circumference plus ½ in. (1.3cm). Cut one 2-in.-wide piece of interfacing or hair canvas the length of the Ultrasuede. Cut two more Ultrasuede pieces the same width as the interfacing but ½ in. longer. One is for the outside of the bracelet and the other is for the lining.

❷ Mark the large Ultrasuede piece as shown in **figure 1** and glue the interfacing to the center on the wrong side. Tie the piece around the round form until dry (**photo a**).

❸ Sew two reinforced, double-thread bead loops to one edge as shown in **figure 1**. The loops need to be long enough to fit over the buttons (**photo b**).

❹ Trim the edge of the interfacing back slightly on the ends and apply glue to the interfacing. Then fold in the sides of the wide piece over the interfacing so they meet in the middle (**photo c**).

❺ Tie the bracelet around the round form again until the glue is dry.

beaded layer

❶ Baste a row of colored thread along the center of one of the Ultrasuede pieces. Then sew the tablet-shaped stone beads in two rows on the bracelet's right side with doubled thread. Leave a small space between each bead and sew them with the bead holes parallel to and oriented toward the centerline (**photo d**).

❷ Using doubled thread, appliqué seed beads across the center of the tablet beads (**photo e**). Come back through half the beads and string enough seed beads to reach the bottom of the tablet, pulling the center strand partway down, as shown in **figure 2** and **photo f**.

❸ Optional: Sew additional accent and seed bead embellishment between or around the tablet beads (**photo g**).

finishing

❶ Glue the lining inside the bracelet, overlapping the button end of the form by about ⅜ in. (1cm) (**photo h**). Sew the buttons near the edge of the overlap to correspond to the loops.

❷ Glue the appliquéd strip to the outside of the form, butting the ends at the loop end (**photo h**). Stretch it tight and glue in stages. If the piece is a tiny bit short because of takeup from the embroidery, the overlap at the button end will hide it. Make sure the layers are well glued at the edges. You can use a head pin to apply tiny amounts of glue at corners and edges. ●—A.K.

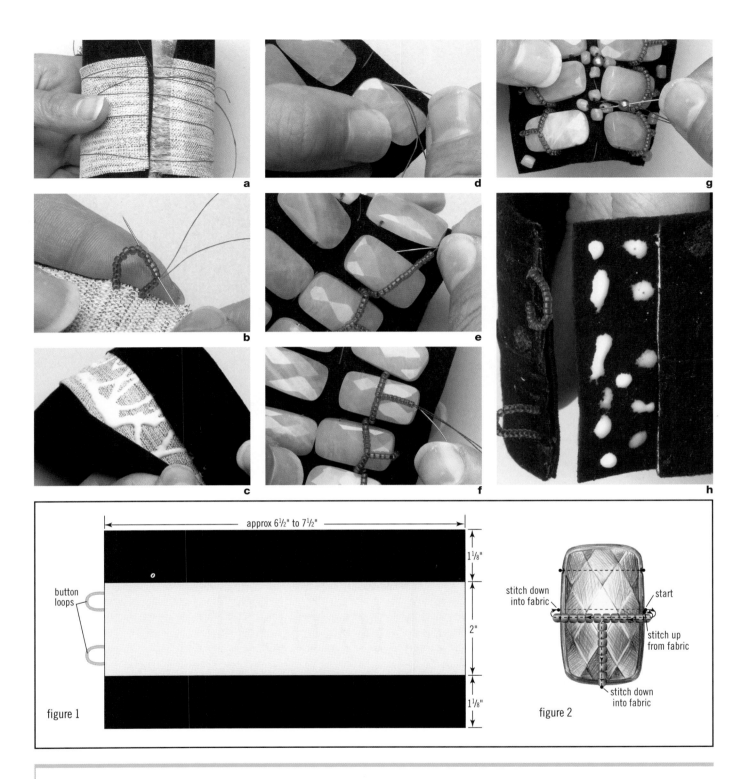

a

b

c

d

e

f

g

h

approx 6½" to 7½"

1⅛"

2"

1⅛"

button
loops

figure 1

stitch down
into fabric

start

stitch up
from fabric

stitch down
into fabric

figure 2

materials

- Ultrasuede or suede leather 10 x 8 in. (25 x 20cm)
- Heavy nonwoven interfacing or hair canvas 2 x 8 in. (5 x 20cm)
- **26-30** 10 x 18mm Tablet-shaped, top-drilled stone beads
- 5-10g Seed beads, size 11º or smaller, contrast or complement to stone beads

- **30-40** Small contrast-color pearl or stone accent beads, optional
- Abrasion-resistant bead cord such as Bitchin' Beads, Power Pro, or Fireline 6 lb. test
- Silamide or Nymo B beading thread
- Beading needles or Sharps, #12 or #13

- **2** Small, flat shank buttons
- White glue or Sobo glue
- Tape measure and glass or jar the same circumference as the bracelet

Basic to bold

One simple technique makes a variety of earrings

If you can turn a loop, you can create an entire wardrobe of earrings in styles ranging from plain and simple to wildly exuberant. Few materials are required, so even the most deluxe earrings are relatively inexpensive to create. Experiment with the three examples offered here and see how far you can go in creating your own variations. When designing earrings, think in terms of the finished weight. You'll want to keep the combination of beads you choose light enough to be comfortable.

The simplest style here—our "basic" —consists of a single bead hung from a finding. The type of bead you choose will determine the look. Go with funky glass, bone, or plastic for a casual daytime look. Choose lustrous pearls, semiprecious stone beads, or sparkling crystals to go from day into evening.

To add movement, enhance the basic style with a dangle below the single bead. For a totally different approach, create a cluster of dangles to hang from the earring finding.

stepbystep

The basic earring consists of a bead strung on a head pin. Make a loop above the bead and hang it on the earring finding. For the basic earring plus dangle, you string the top bead on a leftover piece of head pin or eye pin and make a loop both above and below the bead. Then you string a bead or group of beads on a head pin, make a loop on top, and hang it from the top bead. Hang the assembly on an earring

materials

basic
- **2** Beads
- **2** Flat spacer beads—optional (use with beads that have large holes)
- **2** Head pins, plain or decorated
- Pair of earring findings with a loop

simple dangle
- **2** Medium to large beads
- **2** Head pins, 2 in. (5cm) or longer
- **2** Eye pins—optional (use with short head pins)
- **2-4** Small beads, different shapes and sizes
- Pair of earring findings with a loop

cluster earrings
- **6** in. (15cm) 16- or 18-gauge Sterling silver wire
- **24** or more 2-4mm Beads, pearls, or stone chips
- **24** or more Short silver head pins
- Pair of hoop earring findings

Tools: wire cutter, round- and chainnose pliers; steel block and small smooth-faced hammer for cluster earrings

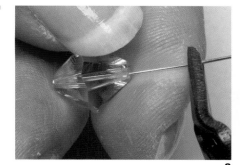

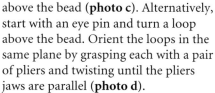

finding. The cluster earring can be a bead with a large loop below and many small beads on head pins attached to it, or in this case, a stiff silver wire with a small top loop and a large bottom loop to hold many single dangle beads.

basic earring

❶ String your bead on a head pin and cut off all but ⅜ in. (1cm) of wire above the bead (**photo a**).

❷ Turn a loop in the wire above the bead (see "Basics," p. 136).

❸ Open the loop sideways (see "Basics") and hook it onto the loop on the earring finding (**photo b**). Then close the loop sideways.

dangle earring

❶ Start the dangle by stringing a bead or group of beads on a head pin. I find that with a group of beads, the earring looks best if the largest bead is on the bottom or in the middle. Cut off all but ⅜ in. of wire and turn a loop against the top bead.

❷ If the leftover piece of wire is the length of the main bead plus ¾ in. (2cm), you can use it for the top bead. Turn a loop on one end of the wire and string the top bead. Then turn a loop

above the bead (**photo c**). Alternatively, start with an eye pin and turn a loop above the bead. Orient the loops in the same plane by grasping each with a pair of pliers and twisting until the pliers jaws are parallel (**photo d**).

❸ Open the loop on the dangle group and attach it to the bottom loop of the main bead (**photo e**). Then close the loop.

❹ Open the loop at the top of the main bead or on the earring finding and link the bead to the finding.

cluster earring

❶ Cut the heavy silver wire into two 2-3-in. (5-7.6cm) pieces and make a loop at each end.

❷ Hammer the shaft of wire between the loops, but don't hammer the loops (**photo f**). Hammering adds hardness, texture, and visual interest.

❸ String one small bead per head pin and make a loop above each. Make 12-

18 dangles for each earring. Because I chose pearls with very small holes, I had to use ultra-thin head pins. (These decorated, single-ball pins are from Bali.) Since the head pins I used were so thin, I opted for wrapped loops for additional security (see "Basics").

❹ If you have plain loops on your dangles, open them and attach each to the bottom loop on the wire shaft. Attach wrapped loops as you make them. When the earring has the fullness you desire, stop adding dangles.

❺ Open the loop on the earring finding and attach the top loop on the wire shaft or slip the top loop onto a hoop finding. ●—*A.K.*

Zigzag floral necklace

This complicated-looking necklace is made with easy daisy-chain stitch

While working on a triangle-stitch necklace and not liking the results, it suddenly hit me that old-fashioned daisy chain, dredged up from my memories of the sixties, would be much more effective for creating the look I wanted. Of course, we have many more wonderful bead colors and shapes today, so these daisies don't look a bit like their sixties' predecessors.

stepbystep

Make a zigzag row of daisies separated by seed beads and pearls. Stabilize the necklace by stringing top and bottom strands through the daisies.

zigzag daisies

❶ Thread a beading needle with a 1-2-yd.- (.9-1.8m) length of bead thread.

❷ Leave an 8-10-in. (20-25cm) tail. Alternate a seed bead and a teardrop 6 times and tie the beads into a tight circle (**figure 1**) with a surgeon's knot (see "Basics," p. 136).

❸ Continue counterclock-wise through the next 7 beads, exiting the 4th seed (**figure 2, a-b**). String a crystal (**b-c**) and go through the first seed bead on the opposite side. Continue clockwise through 6 beads,

exiting the teardrop before the seed where you strung the crystal. Go through the crystal (**d-e**). Enter the first teardrop and continue counterclockwise through the next 7 beads (**e-f**).

❹ String 2 seeds, a pearl, and 2 seeds (**figure 3, a-b**).

❺ Begin the next daisy, the first of the lower row, stringing the 12 daisy beads clockwise, as in **figure 1**. Continue through the first seed (**b-c**), and exit the fourth seed (**c-d**). String a crystal and go through the first seed counterclockwise (**d-e**). Continue through the next 5 beads, exiting the teardrop before the seed where you strung the crystal (**e-f**). Go through the crystal and enter the first teardrop. Continue clockwise through 8 beads, exiting the fourth seed (**g-h**).

❻ String 2 seeds, a pearl, and 2 seeds.

❼ String beads for the next daisy, the second on the upper row. Repeat these steps until you've made 19 daisies. The odd number daisies become the upper row and the even number daisies, the bottom row.

❽ Adjust the daisies so the crystals are on the same side.

necklace strands

❶ Lay the necklace out with the 10-daisy row and the crystals on top.

❷ Cut two 1-yd. (.9m) lengths of bead thread and knot them together at one end with a bulky overhand knot (see "Basics"). Glue the knot and trim the tails when dry. Thread a needle on each cord and take both through a bead tip and a pearl.

❸ Working with the top cord, *string a seed, a silver bead, a seed, and a pearl 4

times. String a seed, a silver bead, and 3 seeds* and go through the top two teardrops and the seed between them on the first top-row daisy (**figure 4, a-b**).

❹ String 3 seeds, a silver bead, 1 seed, a pearl, 1 seed, a silver bead, and 3 seeds and go through the 3 top beads on the next top daisy (**b-c**).

❺ Repeat step 4 until you have connected the tenth top daisy.

❻ Repeat from * to * of step 3, then end with a pearl.

❼ Now string the lower strand: String 3 seed beads, a silver bead, 3 seeds, and a pearl 3 times. Then string 3 seed beads, a silver bead, and 3 seeds (**figure 5, a-b**).

❽ To connect to the necklace, go through the 3 bottom beads on the top row daisy. Go through the next seed bead and the 2 seeds, pearl, and 2 seeds that connect this daisy to the first bottom-row daisy (**b-c**). Follow the path through the lower-edge seed, tear, seed, tear, seed, and tear (**c-d**).

❾ String 7 seeds, a crystal, a seed, a pearl, seed, crystal, and 7 seeds (**d-e**). Go through the bottom 3 beads of the next bottom-row daisy (**e-f**). Repeat through the next-to-last bottom daisy and string **d-e** of this step.

❿ End following the thread path of step 8 in reverse (**figure 5, d-b**). String step 7, **b-a**, and go through the last pearl on the top strand.

⓫ String both needles into a bead tip. Remove slack in the bead strands and string a seed bead on one thread. Then tie several surgeon's knots (see "Basics"). Glue the knots. Trim the tails when dry and close the bead tips.

⓬ Fasten the bead tip hooks to the clasp rings, using roundnose pliers. ●—A.K.

materials

- **114** 3 x 9mm Glass teardrops
- **1** 16-in. (41cm) Strand 7-8mm pearls
- **7g** Seed beads, size 11º
- **36** 2.5-3mm Sterling beads
- **35** 6mm Swarovski crystals
- **2** Sterling silver bead tips
- Clasp
- Fray-resistant bead thread, Bitchin' Beads or Fireline
- Beading needles, #12 or 13
- G-S Hypo Cement
- Beeswax

Tools: chain- and roundnose pliers

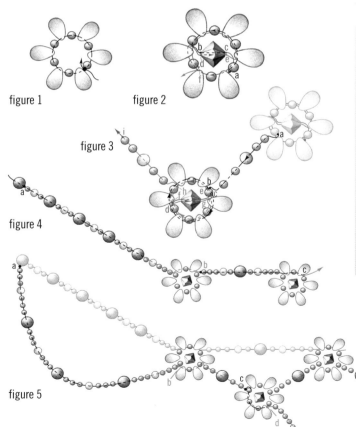

figure 1

figure 2

figure 3

figure 4

figure 5

Winged brooch

Embroider a shimmering butterfly pin

Years ago, I visited Puerto Rico with my husband and was transfixed by the flotillas of butterflies fluttering around the island. We looked in the local shops that sold butterfly specimens in glass cases, but I didn't purchase one. Seeing that magic reduced to a motionless, scientific sample didn't appeal to me. In designing this pin, I've tried to capture the iridescent beauty of my favorite butterfly, the blue morpho. Lepidopterists need not point out the inaccuracies in my rendition. It pleases me to wear this winged brooch knowing that doing so caused no butterfly to meet its end.

stepbystep

This project includes many of Tippy Mueller's embroidery techniques. Her "Hearts in Bloom" brooch appeared in *B&B* #47.

assemble the brooch

❶ Cut four 6 x 6 in. (15 x

15cm) squares of black polyester lining fabric. Use an iron to fuse together two squares with the double-sided interfacing, following the manufacturer's instructions. Fuse the third square to the first two pieces. Repeat with the fourth square.

❷ Use the template (**figure**) provided, or trace a butterfly from a naturalist guide. Cut out the template.

❸ Trace the template onto the fabric with white tailor's chalk (**photo a**).

❹ Use E6000 adhesive to glue the oblong bead into position as the butterfly's body (**photo b**) and allow the glue to dry.

❺ Thread a needle with 2 yd. (1.8m) of Nymo D and begin stitching the wings of the butterfly with beaded backstitch, stitching 3 to 4 seed beads in each stitch (see "Basics," p. 136). The wings are stitched in 3 sections: The top-section stitches are almost horizontal across the wing; the middle-section stitches are sloped at a 45-degree angle from the but-

terfly's body (**photo c**); and the bottom-section stitches are almost vertical. The bead colors change from dark to light, oriented from the body to the wings' edges. Soften the color transitions by adding one darker color bead after the first lighter color bead added in each line of stitching.

❻ Glue the pin finding to the center back of the butterfly (**photo d**).

❼ Cut the Ultrasuede slightly larger than the brooch. Position it over the brooch's back and mark where the ends of the pin finding protrude. Cut round, ¼-in. (6mm) holes at the markings. Reposition the Ultrasuede over the pin finding to make sure the mechanism is not obstructed, and adjust the holes if necessary.

❽ Coat the back of the pin with E6000 adhesive and glue the Ultrasuede in position (**photo e**). Leave a small margin unglued at one edge.

❾ Allow the glue to dry and trim the Ultrasuede so the edges are even (**photo f**).

picot edging

❶ Thread a needle with 4 ft. (1.2m) of Nymo D and tie a

knot near the thread's end. Sew through the Ultrasuede at unglued margin to the pin's back so the knot is between the layers. Stitch back through all the layers from front to back 1⁄16 in. (1.5mm) from the edge. Before tightening the stitch, sew through the thread loop with your needle so the thread comes out straight from the pin's edge.

❷ Pick up a clear silver-lined bead, a black bead, and a clear, silver-lined bead and stitch back to front 1⁄16 in. from the edge and a bead width over from the last stitch. Before tightening the stitch, sew up through the second silver-lined bead.

❸ Pick up a black bead and a silver-lined bead and stitch back to front 1⁄16 in. from the edge and a bead's width over from the last stitch (**photo g**). Sew up through the silver-lined bead before tightening the stitch (**photo h**).

❹ Repeat step 3 to add picot edging along the edge of each wing.

❺ Fold the 8-in. (20.3cm) length of craft wire in half and string a black bead to the center fold.

❻ Thread the wire ends through the art bead from bottom to top. String 13 black beads and 1 silver-lined bead on each wire end. Trim the wire ends so only 1⁄4 in. remains above the beads and turn a small loop with roundnose pliers at each tip (**photo i**). ❍ —*P.O.*

a

g

b

h

c

f

i

materials

- 15g Each of 11º seed beads in silver-lined cobalt blue, silver-lined capri blue, and teal
- 10g Each of 11º seed beads in black and clear silver-lined
- 1 1½ x ½ in. (3.8 x 1.3cm) Oblong art bead
- ¼ yd. (23cm) Black polyester lining fabric
- ¼ yd. Double-sided interfacing
- 1 6 x 6 in. Square of Ultrasuede
- 1 1½ in. Pin back
- 8 in. 24-gauge Craft wire
- E6000 adhesive
- Nymo D
- Beading needles, #10

Tools: iron, roundnose pliers

Interlocking circles

One cross-needle design adapts easily to many styles

After working out the bead counts for the crystal bracelet (above right) I decided to test the flexibility of this cross-needle design by using other types of beads. For the floral bracelet (above left) I worked with vintage-style flowers, fire-polished beads in garden colors, and small leaf beads that dangle off one edge. I created a more tailored look on my third version (opposite), using small pearls for weaving the joined circles and sterling beads in a diamond shape at the crossing points.

stepbystep

Cross-needle weaving can seem awkward at first, although it is an easy technique to master. To steady my work, I simply tape the starting end to my desktop, leaving my hands free to string beads and cross cords. Once a few beads are in place, the design takes shape and the rest of the work goes quickly.

pink crystal bracelet

❶ Cut two 40-in. (1m) lengths of flexible beading wire. Thread each wire through a loop in the clasp and fold the wires in half.

❷ String a 4mm bicone on each pair of wires and push the beads close to the clasp. String another bicone on one strand of wire from either pair. Select one wire from the other pair and go through the bicone from the opposite direction (**figure 1**). Pull the wires apart to tighten the beads.

❸ String three 3mm beads onto each pair of wires. Separate the wires in each pair and designate one outer and one inner wire on each side of the bracelet. String three 3mm beads on each outer wire and two on each inner wire. Cross the inner wires through a 4mm bicone. String two 3mm beads on each of the crossed wires. String the inner and outer wire on each side through a 3mm bead (**figure 2**).

Repeat, following this stringing sequence until the bracelet is the desired length. End with three 3mm beads on each pair of wires. Then cross one wire from each pair through a 4mm bicone.

❹ To add the second clasp half, string a 4mm bicone and a crimp bead on each pair of wires. Thread each pair of wires through a loop on the clasp (make sure the clasp halves fit together correctly when closed) and go back through the crimp and bicone (**figure 3**). Tighten up the beads, crimp the crimps (see "Basics," p. 136), and trim the wires.

floral bracelet

Follow the stringing instructions given above with a few exceptions.

❶ After stringing the clasp, the bud-shaped beads, and the center bead as in steps 1-2, above, string one or two 3mm beads on each pair of wires.

❷ Work the body of the bracelet as in **figure 2**. If you incorporate leaves on one edge, add two or three 3mm beads evenly spaced across the opposite edge. This will keep the bracelet from curving, since the leaves are slightly larger than the 3mm beads they're replacing.

❸ To complete the bracelet, string the second clasp half to match the first, adding crimps as in **figure 3**.

pearl and sterling bracelet

Use 3mm pearls, sterling silver beads, and a magnetic clasp to create a third version of the bracelet. Using a longer bead at the crossing point widens the bracelet slightly and elongates the interlocking circles.

❶ After stringing the clasp, substitute silver spacers and a pearl for the beads in steps 1-2, above. Then string two or three pearls on each pair of wires. Work the body of the bracelet as in **figure 2**. String the second clasp half to match.

❷ Before you add the last few pearls, enlarge their holes slightly with a pearl reamer, if necessary. Then string the clasp and work the beading cord back through the pearls, making several surgeon's knots (see "Basics") as you go. Glue the knots. **❍**—*M.B.*

materials

pink/gray bracelet
- **4** 50-bead Strands 3mm faceted beads
- **1** 50-bead Strand 4mm bicone crystals
- Flexible beading wire, .012 or .013
- **2** Crimp beads
- 2-Strand slide clasp

Tools: crimping pliers

floral bracelet
- **2** 50-bead Strands 3mm fire-polished, faceted beads
- **2** 50-bead Strands 3mm faceted beads, pink
- **10-12** Small glass flowers
- **4** Bud-shaped or narrow flowers
- **9-12** Small leaf-shaped beads
- Fireline fishing line, 6-lb. test
- 2-Strand slide clasp
- G-S Hypo Cement

pearl and sterling bracelet
- **2** 16-in. (40cm) Strands 3mm round pearls
- **13-15** 6mm Sterling silver beads, round, oblong, or diamond-shaped
- Fireline fishing line, 6-lb. test
- Magnetic clasp
- G-S Hypo Cement

Tools: Needle files or bead reamer

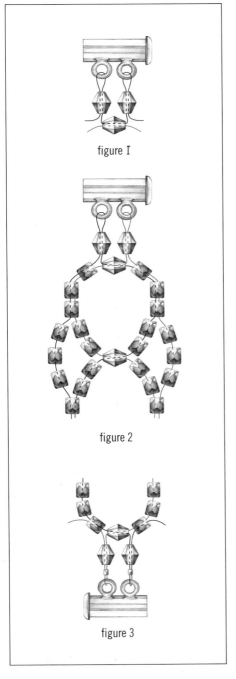

figure 1

figure 2

figure 3

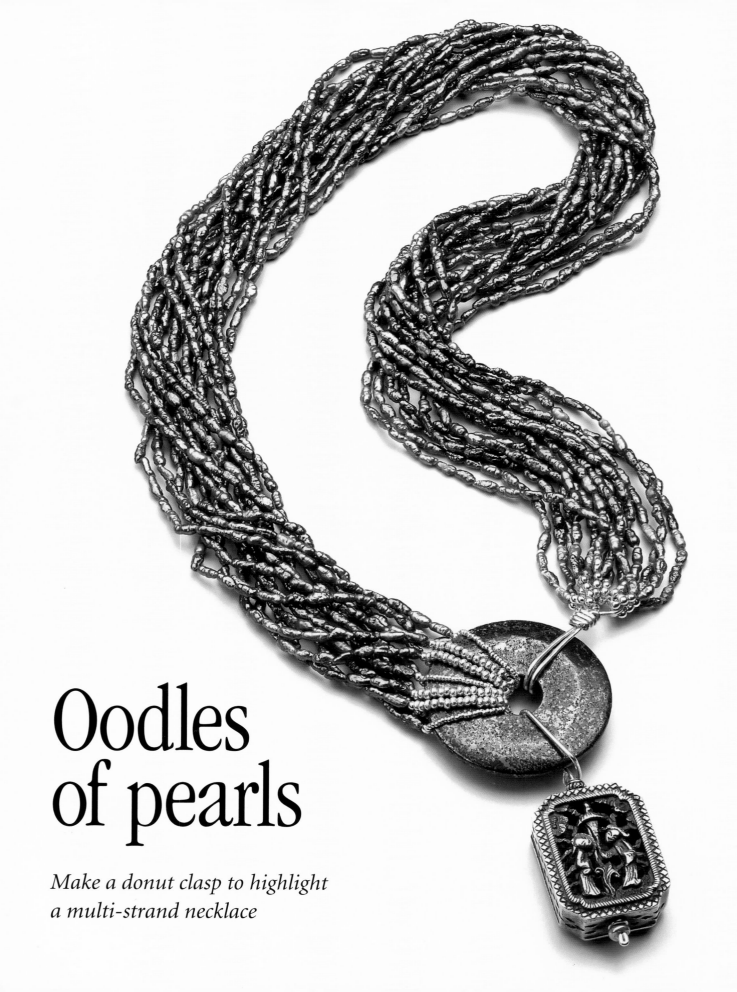

Oodles
of pearls

Make a donut clasp to highlight
a multi-strand necklace

A clasp can make or break the visual impact of a necklace. Interesting clasps are hard to find, however, so it's freeing to be able to make your own. Start by choosing your beads and a large-holed donut that suits them by either coordinating or contrasting in color and pattern. My relatively inexpensive rice-shaped freshwater pearls have so many subtle colors of green, pink, and blue in their silvery-gray luster that I preferred a quiet, unobtrusive pyrite (fool's gold) donut to work with them.

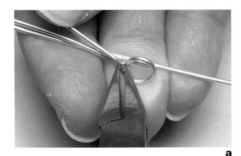

The donut serves as a centerpiece and also provides the loop portion of the clasp. A heavy, hand-made wire hook, hammered for strength, closes the clasp. Without a dangle, this necklace is a tailored, sophisticated piece. Adding the removable dangle can change the entire character of the necklace. Why not make a wardrobe of dangles to suit your many moods?

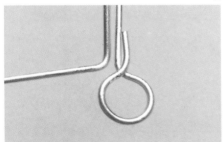

stepbystep

making the hook
❶ Fold the 8-in. (20cm) length of 18-gauge wire in half.

❷ Using the full-size template, p. 134 bottom, bend one leg of the wire at a right-angle to the doubled length and turn a large loop with it. Bend the remainder of the wire at a right angle so the tail is parallel to the doubled shaft (**photo a**). Cut the tail off, leaving about ¼ in. (6mm) (**photo b**).

❸ Bend the long tail at a right angle at the base of the loop (**photo c**).

❹ Grasp all 3 wires in the shaft just above the loop with a pair of flatnose pliers. Using chainnose pliers, wrap the long tail around the 3 wires 3-4 times (**photo d**). If any of the loop wire's tail extends, trim it flush with the last wrap. Cut off the remaining wrap wire and file the end smooth.

❺ Hammer the entire piece on both sides. If the wraps separate a bit, push them back together with pliers.

❻ Measure the amount of shaft you need to go from the edge of the donut to the hole (**photo e**). Use fat roundnose

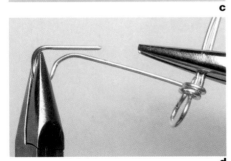

pliers to curve the remainder of the shaft into a hook that will fit around the donut hole (**photo f**).

stringing the necklace
I used two sizes of silver beads to loop the strands around the donut. I simply hadn't bought enough of either size, and the bead store was out of both. Fortunately, they make an attractive combination. To finish the strands as described, you will most likely need to use a file or bead reamer to enlarge the holes on the last 3 pearls strung on each strand.

❶ For the first pair of strands of a 22-in. (51cm) necklace, cut two 70-in.-long (1.8m) cords and thread a needle on each end of each cord.

❷ Holding one needle from each cord together, string one 2mm silver bead, then enough of the tiny silver beads to encircle the donut from hole to edge. Push the beads to the center of the pair of cords and bring the other two needles through the 2mm bead (**photo g**). Four cords and needles now exit this bead.

❸ On each pair of needles, string a

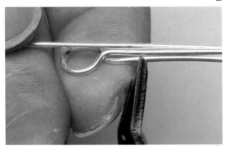

133

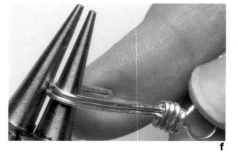

f

k

g

h

i

l

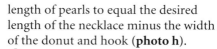

j

m

materials
- **16** 16-in. (41cm) Strands rice-shaped freshwater pearls
- **1** 40cm Stone donut with a large hole (ours is 1cm)
- **10** in. (26cm) approx. 1.5 x 2mm Indonesian silver beads or 2mm round silver beads
- **49** 2mm Round silver beads
- **8** in. (20cm) 18-gauge Round silver wire, half-hard or dead soft
- **1** Spool Bitchin' Beads or Power Pro thin beading thread
- Beading needles, #12 or 13
- G-S Hypo Cement

optional dangle
- **1** Art bead
- **1** Flat sterling silver spacer
- **1** 4mm Sterling silver bead
- **6** in. (15cm) 18-gauge Round sterling silver wire, half hard or dead soft

Tools: roundnose pliers, chain- and flatnose pliers, wire cutters, small metal file, bead reamer, hammer, anvil, steel block, or sidewalk

optional removable dangle

The wire finding I made to attach the dangle to the donut resembles a safety pin and can be easily clipped on or off the donut.

❶ Choose an art bead that looks good with your necklace.

❷ Bend the tip of a 6-in. (15cm) length of 18-gauge wire into a half loop and mash it against the shaft of the wire to form a closed U. String a flat spacer, the art bead, and a 4mm bead.

❸ Line the wire up on the front of the bottom of the donut with the 4mm bead about ¼ in. below the edge of the donut. Mark the point where the wire meets the donut's hole (**photo j**).

❹ Bend the wire around the widest part of your roundnose pliers above the mark. Keep bending until the legs of the wide U above the beads are parallel (**photo k**). Slip the U into the donut to make sure it fits easily and there is still space between the 4mm bead and the bottom of the donut (**photo l**).

❺ Bend the wire tail just above the 4mm bead at a right angle pointing toward yourself. Cut the tail off, leaving about ½ in. (1.3cm), and bend this piece into an open loop that will catch the front of the hanger just above the 4mm bead (**photo m**). ●—A.K.

length of pearls to equal the desired length of the necklace minus the width of the donut and hook (**photo h**).

❹ At the end of a pair of strands, string seven 2mm beads and go through the loop on the hook. Bring two needles through the end pearl on one strand and tie a front-back-front knot after it (see "Basics," p. 136 and **photo i**). Take each needle through the next pearl and tie another front-back-front knot. Repeat once more. End by going through the fourth pearl. Glue all the knots. Repeat this step with the other pair of needles on the other strand.

❺ The necklace shown has 14 strands in seven pairs.

Spiral earrings

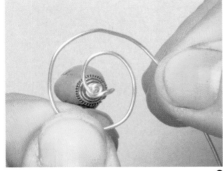

Wrap a wire spiral to energize stone dangles

Sometimes a small flourish makes something plain remarkable. So it is when you add a spiral to ordinary beaded drops.

stepbystep

The shape of your beaded drop should complement the shape of the spiral, so center the large bead and add the smallest beads a

❶ Cut an 8-in. length of 20-gauge wire. Be in. (3mm) at one end and com so it is flat

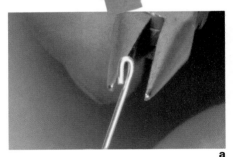

against the length of the wire (**photo a**).
❷ String a small bead, a medium bead, a large bead, a medium bead, and a small bead on the wire.
❸ Make a wrapped loop (see "Basics," p. 136) above the beads (**photo b**). Don't cut off the excess wire.
❹ Curve the remaining wire into a loose coil around the wrapped loop (**photo c**).
❺ After 1½ rotations, pull the coiled wire gently down over the beads (**photo d**). Arrange the wire into a spiral with its

curves spaced evenly along the beaded length of the earring.
❻ Rotate the spiral more tightly around the earring after the midpoint and wrap the wire once between the small bead at the end and the medium bead next to it (**photo e**). Cut the excess wire.
❼ Connect the wrapped loop to the loop on the earring finding (see "Basics"). Close the loop.
❽ Make a second earring to match the first. ❍—*P.O.*

materials

4 1-2mm Beads (small size)
4 4-6mm Beads (medium size)
2 8-10mm Beads (large size)
16 in. (41cm) 20-gauge Wire
2 Earring findings
Tools: chain- and roundnose pliers, diagonal wire cutters

135

basics

figure 1

opening and closing rings

Figure 1: To open a loop or ring, use one or two pairs of pliers to grasp the wire at the opening. Pull one pliers toward you and push the other away to bring the ends of the wire apart and out of the plane of the loop. Never spread the loop side to side, which will fatigue the metal. Close the loop by pulling the sides back into the plane.

figure 2

figure 3

figure 4

making loops or eyes

Figure 2: Cut a head or eye pin, leaving a ⅜-in. (1cm) tail above the bead. Bend it against the bead at a right angle with the tip of a chainnose pliers.

Figure 3: Grip the very tip of the wire in roundnose pliers. If you can feel it when you brush your finger along the back of the pliers, the loop will be teardrop-shaped, rather than round.

Figure 4: Press the pliers downward slightly to avoid pulling and rotate the wire into a loop. Let go, regrasp the loop at the same place on the pliers, and keep turning to close the loop. The closer to the pliers tip that you work, the smaller the loop.

figure 5

figure 6

wrapped loops

Figure 5: Leaving a 1-in. (2.5cm) tail, place the tip of a chainnose pliers against where the bead will be. Bend the tail to form a right angle.

Figure 6: With roundnose pliers, grasp the tail just past the bend and pull it

figure 7

figure 8

figure 9

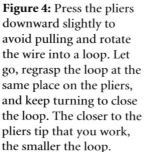

figure 10

over the jaw to point the other way.

Figure 7: Loosen the pliers grip enough to rotate them so the empty jaw is above the partial loop and continue pulling the tail around the bottom jaw until it's perpendicular to the wire.

Figure 8: Pull a split ring, chain, etc., into the loop.

Figure 9: To keep the loop round, grasp it with roundnose pliers in your non-dominant hand above the cross. You can wrap the pliers' jaws with masking tape to avoid denting the wire.

Figure 10: Grasp the tail with chainnose pliers to pull it around the wire until it meets the bead. Make the first wrap against the pliers; keep wraps close together. One wrap is sufficient to keep the loop from opening; additional wraps are decorative. Clip. Then use chainnose pliers to press the cut end against the last wrap.

crimping

Crimping takes two steps.

Figure 11: Thread a crimp bead on one end of a length of flexible beading wire. Then thread one end of the clasp. Bring the wire back through the crimp, leaving a 3-in. (7.6cm) tail. Slide the crimp close to the clasp, leaving a

figure 11

small space. Mash the crimp hard in the hole closest to the handle, which looks like a quarter moon. Hold the wires apart so one piece is on each side of the deep dent.

Figure 12: Put the dented crimp in the front hole of the pliers, standing it on end, and squeeze as hard as you can. This folds the crimp into a small cylinder.

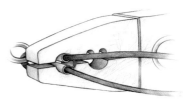

figure 12

bead tips

A bead tip looks like a tiny basket or two half beads with a hooked handle. You use it to hide the knots at the ends of a necklace strand.

Figure 13: Use doubled cord for the bead strand and either tie a fat multiple overhand knot near the end of the tail or tie an overhand knot and string a size 11° seed bead. String through the bead tip from the inside to the outside. Then string the beads.

figure 13

Figure 14: To end, string into a bead tip from the outside. String a size 11º seed bead, then cut off the needle. Tighten the beads on the strand, making sure there are no gaps, but leave enough slack for the strand to drape softly. Then tie the cord ends together with 1-2 surgeon's knots (**figure 27**).

Glue both knots and trim the thread to about ⅛ in. (3mm) when the glue is dry. Press the halves of a bead-style bead tip together with chainnose pliers to enclose the knot and seed bead. Use round-nose pliers to roll the hook tightly closed around the loop on the clasp.

figure 14

pearl knotting

String a knotted necklace on doubled cord, starting with cord four times the desired finished length plus 12 in. (31cm). String a bead tip (if using them), all the beads, and the second bead tip. Push everything that will follow the first knot to the needle end of the cord.

Figure 15: Loop the cord around the first three fingers of your left hand (right for lefties) with the bead tip end on top.

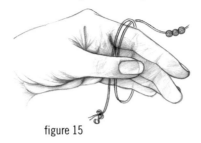

figure 15

Figure 16: Pinch the cross between your thumb and index finger. Hold the cord circle open on your spread fingers with your palm up. Then drop the bead end of the cord through the circle into your hand.

figure 16

Figure 17: Put a long T-pin or an awl into the loop the same way the cord goes through. Gradually tighten the loop as it slips off your fingers, keeping the awl in it. Slide the awl down toward the spot where you want the knot to be as you pull the end of the cord with the loose beads in the opposite direction. When the knot is right against the bead tip or bead, let the cord slip off the tip of the awl. To set the knot, pull the two cord strands in opposite directions. Slide the next bead to the knot and repeat.

figure 17

half-hitch knot

Figure 18: Come out a bead and form a loop perpendicular to the thread between beads in a piece of beadwork or on a strand of beads. Bring the needle under the strand away from the loop. Then go back over the strand and through the loop.

figure 18

double half hitch

Figure 19: Before tightening a half-hitch knot, go through the loop again. Tighten carefully to prevent premature knotting.

figure 19

basics

front-back-front knot

Figure 20: Go through the loop on the clasp. Then thread one needle on each of the two cords. Bring them back through the last bead, one cord at a time. Be careful not to split the cord that is in the bead.

figure 20

Figure 21: Tie the first half of a square knot (**figure 25**) in front of the cord that runs through the strand of beads.

figure 21

Figure 22: Turn the strand over and tie the second half of a square knot (**figure 26**) on the other side of the strand. Turn the strand over once more and tie another half of a square knot in front of the strand.

figure 22

Run both needles through the next bead and make another front-back-

front knot. Go through the third bead and make a final front-back-front knot. End by going through the fourth bead and clip the cord tails. Apply a tiny spot of G-S Hypo cement or clear nail polish to each of the knots for added security.

multiple overhand sliding knot

Figure 23: Place the tail alongside the cord length. Then wrap the tail loosely around both strands, working down toward the loop. Keep the wraps uncrossed. After the last wrap, bring the tail up through the wraps. Tighten it carefully to keep them from crossing. Pull the cord length to tighten the loop.

figure 23

overhand knot

The easiest way to tie an overhand knot is to wrap the cord over your hand. **Figure 24:** Make a loop in the cord and bring the end that crosses on top behind the loop. Then pull it through to the front.

figure 24

square knot

Figure 25: Bring the left-hand cord over the right-hand cord and around.

figure 25

Figure 26: Cross the right-hand end over the left and go through the loop.

figure 26

surgeon's knot

A surgeon's knot is a stronger version of a square knot. Its extra wrap makes the top curl around the sides.
Figure 27: Begin as a square knot: left over right and around then right over left and through (**figures 25 and 26**). Go through the loop again, then tighten.

figure 27

lark's head knot

A lark's head knot is commonly used to start macrame.

Figure 28: Fold a cord in half at the middle and put the fold through a ring or loop from front to back. Slip the tails through the fold loop from front to back and tighten.

figure 28

right angle weave

Figure 29: To start the first row, string 4 beads and tie the thread into a snug circle. Pass the needle through the first 3 beads again. (Maintain a firm tension to form the distinctive cross shape.)

figure 29

Figure 30: Pick up 3 more beads (#5, 6, and 7) and sew back through the last bead of the previous circle

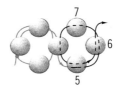

figure 30

and beads #5 and 6.

Figure 31: Pick up 3 more beads and sew back through #6 and the first 2 new beads. Continue adding 3 beads for each stitch until the first row is the desired length. You are sewing circles in a figure-8 pattern and alternating direction with each stitch.

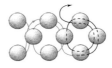

figure 31

Figure 32: To begin row 2, sew through the last 3 beads of the last stitch on row 1, exiting the bead at the edge of one long side.

figure 32

Figure 33: Pick up 3 beads and sew back through the bead you exited in figure 31 (the first "top" bead of row 1) and the first new bead of row 2.

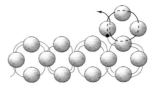

figure 33

Figure 34: Pick up 2 beads and sew back through the next top bead of the previous row and the last bead of the previous

stitch. To begin the next stitch, sew through the next top bead of row 1.

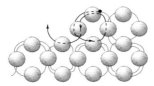

figure 34

To work the next stitch, you'll pick up 2 beads, sew through the side bead of the previous stitch, the top bead of the row below, and the first new bead. The thread is moving in the same direction as it did in **figure 33**.

Keep the thread moving in a figure-8, alternating the patterns of **figures 33 and 34**. Pick up 2 beads for each of the remaining stitches on the row. Don't sew in straight lines between stitches.

beaded backstich

Figure 35: To stitch a line of beads, come up through the fabric from the wrong side. String three beads. Stretch the bead thread along the line where the beads will go, and go through the fabric right after the end bead. Come up through the fabric between the second and third beads and go through the third bead again. String 3 more beads and repeat. For a tighter stitch, string only one or two beads at a time. ●

figure 35

tips & techniques

Stringing

sealing nylon knots

Instead of tying knots on nylon thread (such as Nymo), you can melt the thread to form a secure end. Cut the Nymo about 1/16 in. (1.5mm) from the end of your beadwork. Bring the flame of a disposable lighter near the thread end until the thread shrivels into a small ball and disappears into the nearest bead. Just use the flame's heat. If you use the flame itself, you'll get an ugly burned ball. You can also melt a knot onto the starting end of a thread this way. *–Nicole Campanella*

sealing a knot

To seal a knot, put a small amount of nail polish or glue on the tip of your needle. Touch the needle's tip to the knot, covering it with glue. Let dry. This tip comes from a workshop with Virginia Blakelock. *–Denise Hofmann*

fixing stringing mistakes

I like to make large woven tapestries and patches for jacket backs on my 25 x 25-in. (63 x 63cm) loom. A stringing error is a real problem, so here's how I avoid it, providing my thread is at least three times as long as the distance back to my mistake. This will work for necklaces, too.

In the first photo, the two black beads are supposed to be red, so reinsert the needle back along the row, coming out just after the black beads. Don't pull all the way through and be careful not to split the thread. Leave a big loop on the edge and hold it with your little finger for safety. Pick up the correct beads (two red ones) and thread the needle back through all the other correct beads to the loop on your finger. Pull the thread from both ends, and the bad beads will drop off and be replaced by the new ones. *–Roy E. Garvie*

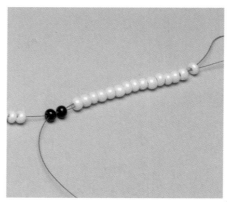

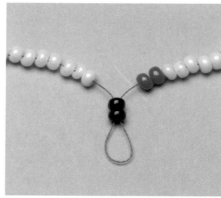

more on fixing stringing errors

When I noticed a small mistake in a complicated sequence of strung beads, I thought I'd have to spend hours taking the necklace apart to repair the error. So, I came up with this alternative approach. I slid a short length of thin beading wire through the section I had to remove to reach my error and transferred the beads in order. Then, I fixed the problem and slid the beads back onto the original wire. By keeping the strung beads in order, the repair took a fraction of the time. *–Pam Overton*

fitting a multi-strand necklace

After some frustrating moments getting multi-strand necklaces to drape well, I devised a way to test the drape before I finish a piece. String all the strands the same length, then curve them into the rounded shape of a neckline. Add beads to each side of the outer strands until you have a V-shape across the top. String crimps and the clasp as though you were going to finish the necklace. Fold a piece of tape tightly around each wire end to prevent any movement in the stringing. Try on your necklace and make any shaping adjustments simply by removing the tape to add or subtract beads. *–Emily Quinn*

Needles

get it over early

My favorite beading tip came from Suzanne Cooper, who got it from a student in one of Barb Grainger's classes. Thread about 20 needles on your spool. Then, as you need more thread, just take a needle with the length of thread you need. Voila! *–Diane Ekhammer*

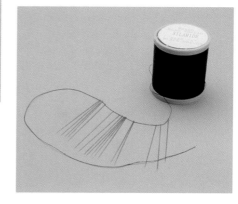

needle facts

English beading needles usually bend easily (but don't break easily), while Japanese needles are stiff but brittle. You'll find different uses for each type. But beware—their sizes are numbered in opposite directions. An English #16 is the smallest size and a Japanese #16 is the biggest. —*Diane Fitzgerald*

Thread
extra-long thread

I hate to run out of thread when I'm beading, so I've started using an extra-long piece, about 10 ft. (3m) or more. I put a stop bead in the middle and work from the middle out. When I run low on thread, I simply remove the stop bead and begin working in the opposite direction. This works well for spiral rope chain, heirloom lace, and other symmetrical patterns. To secure a stop bead on thread, position the bead and run the thread through it twice in the same direction. Wind the long non-working thread end around a small card to keep it from tangling. —*Susan Forbes*

new beading filament

It's no secret that manufacturers of fishing supplies also produce great products for beaders. So on a recent trip to a sporting goods store, I bought several kinds of fishing line to try. My new favorite for both stringing and weaving is Fireline by Berkley. It comes in a neutral gray color, doesn't tangle easily, doesn't stretch, threads effortlessly, and holds up well to beads with sharp or rough edges. I use glue to keep the knots from slipping. —*Robin Moore*

Bead crochet
crocheted bangle bracelet

To create the distinctive look of this crocheted bracelet, string a repeating pattern of three 6ºs and six 8ºs on a sturdy cord such as Conso #18. Crochet the rope (*B&B* #41), working nine beads around. Putting a twist-tie in the rope's

core helps support the beads and keeps the circle clearly defined as you crochet. Connect the ends by sewing back and forth between the first and last row of beads. Line up the colors carefully so your finished bracelet has two continuous spirals. —*Carolee Rand*

beads on variegated thread

Not long ago, a friend sent me a spool of variegated thread as a gift. After a little experimentation, I found a wonderful way to use it in my beaded crochet ropes. I strung the thread with clear 11º beads in gloss and matte finishes. Bands of color show through the transparent beads, and the effect is beautiful. —*Judith Griffin*

Beadweaving
peyote with pony beads

A good way to get children started with peyote stitch is to use pony beads and elastic thread. It's an ideal way to make fun bracelets, especially for preteens. The elastic's stretchiness makes it quite forgiving. —*Samantha Lynn*

easy ladder-stitch start

Here's an easy way to make a ladder when you're starting a piece in brick stitch. String the required number of beads. Go back through the second bead from the needle in the same direction as the first pass. Pull the thread tight and coax the beads to lie side by side. Continue this way through each bead, always passing the thread toward the

needle end. When you're done, you can reinforce the ladder by working your thread up and down through the beads. I find this method less confusing than building a ladder one bead at a time, especially when the ladder contains a color pattern. —*Loris*

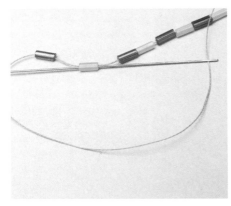

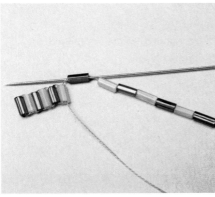

controlling long threads

When working on a peyote project, I estimate the length of thread I'll need and unwind half that amount from the spool. Then I thread my needle—without cutting the thread off the spool—and string my beads, starting in the middle of the project. The spool keeps the beads from falling off. When I finish the first half, I unwind more thread and continue on the other half. I save time and I don't need the stop bead. —*Catherine M. Picheniuk*

starting amulet bags

When I start a peyote-stitch amulet bag, I string the first circle of beads in a contrasting color. Then I go through all

tips & techniques

the beads and a few more again, pulling on the tail and working thread to make the circle tight. After I stitch several rows, I pull out the starting beads. This method gives me good tension at the top of the purse. –*Anne Manninen*

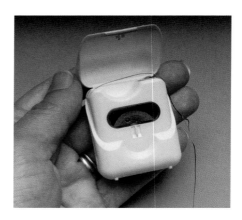

Organization and storage
recycling dental floss containers
Dental floss containers are the perfect size to hold spools of Nymo thread, and with a built-in cutter, you don't have to look for scissors. They keep the thread from unwinding, too. I mark the size and color on the front of the container. –*Idele Gilbert*

color samples
If you want to see how different colors of beads will look together in beadwork, make small peyote-stitch samples for each color. Mine are 10 beads wide, one inch (2.5cm) long, and tapered at one

end with a loop so that samples can be kept on a ring. You can lay the swatches side-by-side to see how the colors work together. –*Diane Fitzgerald*

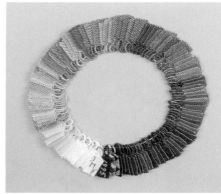

secure bead carrier
A portable CD case makes a great carrier when you're traveling with beads. Remove the plastic insert from a CD case and slide a stiff piece of cardboard into the pockets in the front and back covers. Cut two pieces of thin foam to fit inside the case and press a ceramic bead dish into the bottom piece. Now when you close the case, the top piece of foam will fit tightly against the bead dish, and your traveling beads will stay in their respective compartments. –*Carol Perrenoud*

divided bead tray
When I'm working with several colors or kinds of beads that I don't want to mix in one pan, I use an inexpensive ceramic Japanese ink tray from an art supply store. It has six depressions. If I need more spaces or the beads are large I use a muffin pan. –*Sarah Brodsky*

beads under wraps
After spilling more than a few saucers of loose beads, I began using a new Saran Wrap product to cover my bowls when they're not in use. Quick Covers are plastic lids that look like small shower caps. They keep the beads in and the dust and cats out. –*Susan Helmer*

handy thread storage
My thread supply was always tangled until I discovered prescription medicine bottles that are the exact size of my spools and bobbins. Since any bare surface is fair game for a beaders, I covered one bottle in tubular peyote. Then I did one in 3-bead netting and one in Ndebele herringbone. To finish each container, I glued a pincushion onto the lid to keep my extra needles visible and off the floor. –*Rebecca Bell*

Beads, etc.
removing rust from glass beads
If you use steel mandrels, try a rust-removing toilet bowl cleaner to remove rust stains from your glass beads. Use rubber gloves and a glass container and be careful. A quick soak of a few minutes, an old toothbrush, and a good rinse will do the trick. If you soak the beads too long, they will etch somewhat. It's a nice effect if that's what you want. –*Bruce Cutean*

bead rings
Put 20 seed beads of one color onto a head pin and form a loop at the top. Then string it onto a heavy-gauge wire ring. Repeat this for each color of seed bead you own. (Carry the ring in your purse. You never know when you'll find a bead store.) When you're running low on a color, wrap a piece of tape around the head pin so you'll remember to restock it. The ring is also a good way to play with different color combinations. –*Sharon Lester*

running out of beads

If I see that I won't have enough of a seed bead color to finish a project and I can't find more beads that match exactly, I start randomly blending in more and more of the new close match. By the time I run out of the original color, I've switched to the new color. If I do it right, the transition doesn't show at all or it looks planned. *–Sarah Ferber*

great surface for beads

A material that's wonderful to bead on is Velux, a synthetic fabric often used for blankets. You can cut the material to fit a tray or any other working surface. It's machine washable, and the nap keeps beads from rolling around. Inexpensive twin-size Velux blankets are available at discount stores. Buy one and cut it into pads for yourself and your beading friends. *–Amy Bradley*

Wirework
double loops

Use a double loop in place of any single loop in your jewelry. It resembles a split ring and offers greater security. Place the tip of your chainnose pliers 1 in. (2.5cm) from the end of a piece of wire or head pin. Bend, forming a right angle. Grip the very tip of the wire in roundnose pliers as you would when making a plain loop. Without pulling, rotate the wire into a loop. Let go and regrasp the loop at the same place on the pliers. Keep rotating to close the first loop. To form the second loop, keep rotating, making sure that the second loop is made next to the first. *–Theresa Schwab*

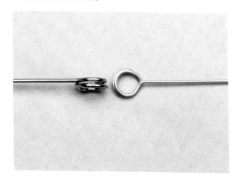

tarnishing silver

Instead of using a commercial product to tarnish or darken my sterling silver jewelry projects, I simply drop the silver into a plastic storage bag with a hard-boiled egg cut in half. The egg releases sulfur that works as effectively as the chemicals, but it takes a few hours instead of a few seconds. To make sure the silver is evenly exposed to the sulfur gas, shake the bag a few times during the process. *–Nicolette Stessin*

cut wire safely

If you don't wear eyeglasses or own a pair of safety glasses, here's a simple way to protect your eyes while cutting wire. Hold the wire and wire cutters inside a gallon-size plastic storage bag. The bag is clear so you can see what you're doing, and it will prevent the cut pieces from flying toward your face. *–Mary Head*

Miscellaneous
pick 'em up

Seed bead spills are no fun, but this is one tried-and-true way to get back to beading. Use a rubber band to fasten a piece of old pantyhose or thin fabric firmly over the nozzle of your vacuum cleaner rod. The vacuum will suck the beads onto the cloth without pulling them into the bag. *–Heather Avery*

glued findings

After I glue earrings or pendants, I place them in an old candy box filled halfway with rice. The rice supports the findings so they don't move, and when the lid is closed, I don't have to smell the glue. *–MABeads*

napkin rings and wine glass ID tags

Small-diameter (ring-sized) memory wire is just right for making napkin rings and stemware markers. Cut off 4-in. (10cm) lengths for napkin rings and 3-in. (7.6cm) lengths for stemware markers using industrial-strength wire cutters or grasp the wire where you

want to break it with chainnose pliers and bend it back and forth. Start with a small loop on one end. String the wire with beads and finish with another small loop. Make each a different color or add a small dangle or charm to the loop as an identifier. *–Nancy Waters*

perfectly matched earrings

Here's how I get earring lengths to match perfectly: Thread the beads on one head pin or eye pin. Leave room for a loop and cut off the extra length above the beads. Use that piece to measure an identical cut on the other pin. *–Maureen Murray*

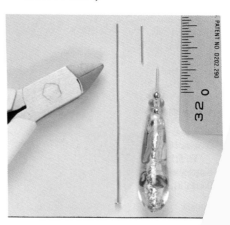

beads in bowls

Instead of using a watercolor tray my beads, I use shallow soy sauce I like keeping one bead color in bowl, and I can move them aro work. *–Deb Atkinson*

INDEX

A

Art beads, 22, 121, 101, 133
Awl, 9

B

Bead ribbons, 99
Bead appliqué, 122
Bead embroidery, 119, 128
Bead tips, 8, 136
Bead weaving, 97
Beaded backstich, 139
Beaded handbag
 The personal touch, 119
Bracelets
 Appliqué cuff, 122-123
 Asymmetry in stone, 108-110
 Beaded bangles, 84-85
 Beaded links, 66-67
 Classic multi-strand bracelets, 38-40
 Delicate dangle bracelets, 112-113
 Elegant pearl lattice, 78-79
 Graceful geometrics, 52-54
 Interlocking circles, 130-131
 Lasso your wrist, 50-51
 Liquid silver jewelry ensemble, 102-104
 Make your own tennis bracelet, 30-31
 Mini-pearl dangle bracelet, 25
 Simply linked, 105
 Tall or short, 14-15
 Time on a beaded strand, 20-21
 Understated elegance, 106-107
 Unforgettable bracelets, 60-61
 Woven stone cuff, 96-97
Braiding, 39-40
Brick-stitch, 58-59
Brooches. *See* Pins

C

Calottes. *See* bead tips
Chain, 18, 28, 57, 76, 77, 99, 105, 115
Chainnose pliers, 9
Charms, 42, 51, 55, 60, 111
Clasps, 8
 interesting, 133
 making your own, 133
Cones, 8, 42, 65
 showcasing 121
Cord, 8
Crimp beads, 8
 mping, 136
  ing pliers, 9
   edle weaving, 52-54, 130

    stitch, 127
   5, 28, 29, 41, 44, 50, 55, 57, 70, 77, 81,
    117, 124, 133, 135
    s, 9

    110

Earrings, cont.
 Cone classics, 65
 Diamond ball earrings on a budget, 70-71
 Falling leaves, 116-118
 Fine feathered friends, 82-83
 Hoop dangles, 29
 Hoops are hot, 11
 Liquid silver jewelry ensemble, 102-104
 Mix and match, 111
 Pearl ribbons, 99
 Spiral earrings, 135
 Teardrop earrings, 87
Ethnic flavor, 42, 75, 89, 97
Eye pins, 8, 67

F

Feathers, 83
Findings, 8
Flatnose pliers, 9
Flexible beading wire, 8
Foxtail, 115
Fringe, 58

H

Head pin, 8
Heirloom lace, 15
Hoops, 11, 29, 85

I

Indian bead loom, 97

J

Jump rings, 8

K

Knotting
 awl, 37, 91
 double half hitch, 137
 front-back-front, 137
 half-hitch, 137
 Lark's head, 139
 multiple overhand sliding, 137
 overhand, 138
 pearl, 37, 137
 silk, 62
 square, 138
 surgeon's, 138
 with tweezers, 62-63

L

Lampwork beads, 22-24
Lariats
 bracelet, 50
 Create a lariat with pizzazz, 80-81
 Lariats, a fashion basic, 26-27
Lattice-style jewelry, 78-79
Leather, 122
Loops
 making, 136
 opening and closing, 136

M

Memory wire, 9, 14, 60, 113
Memory wire bracelets, 14-15, 60, 113

N

Necklace spreaders, 89, 107
Necklaces
 A new look at foxtail, 114-115
 Assymetry in stone, 108-110
 Beaded links, 66-67
 Caged beads, 48-49
 Chained elegance, 56-57
 Contemporary accents, 100-101
 Create a lariat with pizzazz, 80-81
 Create a Tribal Look 75-76
 Drop everything!, 18-19

Necklaces, cont.
 Easy as 1-2-3, 68-69
 Elegant neckwires, 90-91
 Falling leaves, 116-118
 Fine feathered friends, 82-83
 Graceful geometrics, 52-54
 Hooked on pearls, 120-121
 Italian designer necklace, 10-12
 Keep it simple, 16-17
 Knot hard, 62-63
 Lariats, a fashion basic, 26-27
 Liquid silver jewelry ensemble, 102-104
 Making odd ends meet, 42-43
 multi-strand, 11, 16, 22, 35, 69, 73, 75, 89, 101,
  108, 121, 132
 Oodles of pearls, 132-134
 random-patterned, 42-43
 Shimmer aplenty, 34-35
 Show it off, 36-37
 Showcasing lampwork beads, 22-24
 Strand multiplication, 88-89
 String a vintage look, 46-47
 Summer spirals, 72-73
 Understated elegance, 106-107
 Use French wire, 64
 What to do with leftover beads, 44-45
 Y Wonder, 94-95
 Zigzag floral necklace, 126-127

P

Pendants
 Italian designer necklace, 10-12
 tassel, 46
Pins
 Pin frills, 58-59
 Winged brooch, 128-1129

R

Right-angle weave, 31, 138
Rings
 Half-round Roman ring, 93
Roundnose pliers, 9

S

Spacer bars
 creating, 78, 103
Split rings, 8
Stringing, 8-9, 36-37

T

Tassels
 beaded, 46-47, 94
 fiber, 47
Thread snips, 9
Toggles, 40, 81
Tools, 9
Tweezers, 61
Twisted wire needles, 9

U

Ultrasuede, 59, 97, 122, 128

W

Watch, 20-21
Wire, 9
 bending, 32-33, 91, 93
 bullion, 64
 French, 64
 wrapping, 49, 91, 93, 135
Wire bobby pins, creating, 23
Wrapped loops, 18, 25, 28, 44, 49, 65, 73, 83, 135, 136

Y

Y-necklace, 94-95

or
owls.
ch
d as I